G000254138

Mo.
Haunted
Island

Isle of Wight Ghosts
Book Six

Gay Baldwin

visit
www.ghost-island.com
for new stories

CHAPTERS

INTRODUCTION

Welcome to this Most Haunted Island, the book I wasn't going to write. Five books about ghosts on the Isle of Wight were quite enough, I thought. No one will want to read a sixth book! But the stories kept on coming. There are so many fascinating and incredible accounts of ghosts and hauntings, that this is my biggest book so far.

To those people who have shared their experiences with me, thank you so much. And to those of you whose stories I haven't yet used because I ran out of space, don't despair. You will be able to read some of them on my Ghost Island website at: www.ghost-island.com instead.

Far from diminishing, interest in the paranormal seems to increase with the years. People today are far more willing to keep an open mind about the possibility that ghosts might and **do** exist. Most of us are fascinated by the supernatural. Sixty percent of people in Britain now believe in ghosts, and your chance of seeing one is estimated at one in ten. Just like us, every ghost, spirit, phantom or spectre is different. They include:

> **Historical ghosts**. These are traditionally associated with old castles and ancient buildings. Events are imprinted on the atmosphere or surroundings and replayed like a psychic video recording to people receptive to it. Over time these fade like a battery running down.
> **Regular ghosts**. Some hauntings follow cycles, reappearing on a certain date or time of year in a regular pattern. Atmospheric conditions or changes in the magnetic field may play a part in these appearances.
> **Poltergeists**. Their activity is often centred around a particular person in a household; frequently an adolescent, and disturbances, noises, throwing or disappearance of objects may be an unconscious case of mind over matter.
> **Crisis apparitions**. Usually ghosts of the newly-dead, they are seen for a few days at most. The spirit of a loved one visiting for a last farewell is by far the commonest type of apparition.

What is a ghost? A ghost or spirit is the life force of someone who has died, but not ceased to exist in this realm. Often they are spirits or souls of those who have died violently or suddenly. Others are trapped on the earth plane, not accepting they have died; or have become lost on their way to the afterlife. Some have such strong ties to the living, or their old life that they won't leave. Their dimension is timeless and if contacted through psychics, these spirits are surprised how long they've been "dead".

Who can see ghosts? Almost anyone it seems. You don't have to believe in them to see one. Children and animals often see ghosts.

What does a ghost look like? Some appear solid and real, while others are wispy and ethereal. Some resemble a reflection in a plate glass window; others consist of dots or sparks of energy. Ghosts can also be heard or smelled, some have been photographed and a few whisper, moan or talk.

Why do ghosts appear? There's often an obvious explanation for a haunting like murder, suicide or violent death. Tragedy, unhappiness or despair leaves its imprint on a place, lingering in the atmosphere like a psychic recording, to be replayed at intervals when conditions are right or someone receptive comes along. Perhaps what we call 'ghosts' are spirits on a wavelength different to our own. Does our undying mind carry an energy, which, after death, becomes part of the energy pattern of its surroundings?

Do haunted houses have memories? Do ghosts walk when no one is there to see them or must they draw on our energy fields to materialise, making us shiver when they're around? When a ghost is seen walking through a 'solid' wall, can we believe our eyes? Perhaps. For our solid-seeming world of matter is actually energy vibrating at different wavelengths. When defining matter, Albert Einstein described it as "congealed light". Taken to their ultimate, matter and energy are one and the same.

So do ghosts exist, albeit in a dimension or on a wavelength different to our own? I believe that they do. I have, over the years, interviewed many hundreds of people from all walks of life, who have seen, heard, felt, or even smelled ghosts. Some of the strange events and occurrences would be all but impossible to make up. Now I challenge you to read these stories and make up your own mind.

"There is something marvellous beyond the horizon of death and the limit of our sight. It becomes personal knowledge when our minds are coaxed out of the shadows of the purely material world and into the brilliance and brightness of the world of spirit... that lies just beyond the limit of our sight."

H.P.Lovecraft

The ghosts of Roman soldiers have been seen on the Island

Chapter One

ROMAN REMAINS AND GHOSTS OF VECTIS

Here on the Isle of Wight are ever-present reminders of a time, almost twenty centuries ago, when Romans occupied the Island. In 43AD the 5,000 strong Second Legion under its 34-year-old leader, Vespasian, took over the Island in the name of Rome. They called it Vectis - and this name can still be seen on many businesses today – including the local bus company, Southern Vectis.

The population which numbered only a few hundred, put up little or no resistance to the highly-trained and disciplined Roman soldiers. Over the next 400 years, the Romans set about establishing themselves, creating prosperous farms and villas. Traces of their occupation are scattered throughout the Island and remains of villas have been found at a number of sites, including Brighstone, Clatterford, Carisbrooke, Combley, Bowcombe and Gurnard. The best preserved villas, which are now open to the public, were discovered at Newport and Brading, where the latter, built towards the end of the Second century AD, has 12 living rooms, a bathroom suite and hot air central heating. Fine mosaics show it was a dwelling of taste and elegance.

Although pottery, jewellery and hoards of coins have also been found, no trace of any straight, well-drained and engineered Roman road has yet been discovered, although on the Island's range of chalk hills known as the Downs, are stretches of ancient highway which were used long before the Romans came.

The Roman occupation ended around AD 410 when the Legions were ordered back to Rome to defend their homeland. Although they had protected the civilian inhabitants from war and invasion for centuries, the Roman military forces were continually fighting. Life had become increasingly hard, with armed raids by Jutes, Angles and Saxons. The departure of the Legions signalled a bloody end to peace and prosperity. The Dark Ages had arrived.

SOLDIER GHOSTS

None of this, however, was on the mind of Phil Surridge when he took his two dogs, Sieger, a 15-year-old German Shepherd and Tyson, a

Belgian Shepherd rescue dog, for a walk on Brading Down one Saturday morning in January 2003.

Phil, who lives in Binstead, is a former fireman and a retired prison officer, who now has time to indulge his passion for playing Fifties and Sixties rock and roll music with his group 'Kommotion'.

"It was about 11.30am on January 25, a fine, bright morning, when I parked my van in the smaller car park at the side of the Downs road, went through the gate and started walking towards Brading along one of the ridge paths," he said.

After about a quarter-of-a-mile, Phil saw a woman with a dog coming towards him. As Tyson had a nervous disposition, Phil turned back. The dogs ran on ahead towards the van.

"After walking a short way, it was then that I had the feeling of someone alongside me. Out of the corner of my eye I saw a movement and looked sideways. There, just a couple of feet away, I could see what looked like a Roman soldier, but quite solid and real. He was wearing yellow-brown leather sandals and his bare legs were dusky brown. He had a wine-coloured skirt under brown leather straps, the ends of which were decorated with yellow metal like brass.

"I could also see a brown, leather belt and the bottom half of an oblong, thick leather shield. This was also brown in colour, edged with yellow metal or brass, which was being held on his left side. Above the waist the figure seemed to fade, but it was not a sharp change. I had a strange feeling - although I can't prove any of this - that although I only saw one figure, I was walking among a formation or troop of soldiers.

"I could hear a noise as though a sword was knocking against the shield and I was conscious of the tramping of footsteps, a jingling noise and the movement of uniforms around me.

"The figure stayed alongside me for some distance, between ten and 15 paces – but it was like everything was happening in slow motion. I held my breath and turned around to face the figure. As I moved, everything disappeared. There was nothing and no-one around. I called my dogs back to see if they could sense anything strange, but they were more interested in getting back in the van.

"When I reached the van I put the dogs in and just sat in the driver's seat. I felt shell-shocked. My head and my heart were pounding as I mentally asked dozens of questions of myself, none of which I could answer. I was not frightened, I was spooked! After a while I started to look around and back to where I had been walking. It was then that I glanced over towards the Brading Roman Villa. It was the first time I had made the connection. Perhaps it was wishful thinking or I was trying to make sense of something that just couldn't have happened.

"I have retraced my steps several times since that day, walking my dogs on the Downs, hoping for another experience. Nothing has happened yet. It's just a lovely place to be and to enjoy. There is no way I can prove that anything happened that day. I just know what I saw, felt and heard."

ROMANS RETURN

Several months after Phil gave me details of this experience, he had another incredible encounter with the paranormal on Brading Down, which he can still hardly believe.

It was 7.30pm on 4 August 2003, when Phil went for a walk in the warmth of the early evening sun accompanied by Tyson. Sadly, Sieger had died a few months earlier. This time, Phil was walking away from the car park towards Brading with the dog trotting along behind him, admiring the views out to sea. Suddenly Tyson let out a startled yelp, whimpered, and lay down with his paws in front and head to one side.

Startled by the dog's strange behaviour, Phil stopped and looked around. There, in front of him, less than twenty yards away, was a group of eight Roman soldiers, standing in two rows of four.

An incredulous Phil told me, "I couldn't believe it had happened again. I told myself I must be imagining it – that wishful thinking was causing me to conjure them up. It was like I was being greedy to see something again, but my eyes were drawn to them like a magnet."

He quickly glanced down at Tyson who was still lying in the same curious pose, staring intently, right at the phantom soldiers. Looking back at the ghosts, Phil half expected them to have disappeared. But there they were, standing as if 'at ease', appearing real and solid. This time their entire bodies were visible and Phil could see all the elements of the soldiers' uniforms - from their sandal-clad feet to headgear of dark leather helmets topped with bright red plumes. He quickly scanned the figures, looking for details that had not been evident on the earlier sighting.

"The underskirts were that same distinctive mauve-wine colour. It is so unusual that I registered it immediately. This time I could see they were wearing leather breastplates, and there was fabric around the necks and sleeves in the same vivid colour as the underskirts.

"All eight had swords strapped in leather scabbards which hung almost to knee length. They were holding dark, leather shields on their left and in their right hands were what looked like spears or pikes. On their heads were dark, leathery helmets with short bright red plumes going from front to back. The helmets were held in place by leather straps under the chin."

The soldiers, who were neither particularly young nor old, were totally unaware of Phil and Tyson, or their 21st century surroundings. "Last time I was walking amongst them, but now I was able to stand back and observe everything about them. They remained visible for a minute or so, but curiously, during that time everything was silent and still. No traffic passed on the road, and nobody else was about. I noticed that the soldiers appeared to be following the same path as last time."

Twice, Phil looked down to check on Tyson, who remained transfixed by the ghostly figures. "All this time I was standing near a picnic table set in concrete, gazing at something that my logical mind told me couldn't be happening. However, I wasn't brave enough to get any closer and Tyson made no move towards them either. The next time I took my eyes off them, they vanished. Suddenly, everything was back to normal. I was aware of cars passing, and the dog was ready to resume his walk."

So what happened that balmy summer's evening on Brading Down? Was Phil's sense of unfinished business playing on his imagination sufficiently for his subconscious mind to summon up the apparitions? Did wishful thinking play its part in bringing the soldiers back from the dead? Perhaps.

But what of Tyson? Dogs may be woefully ignorant of Roman history but they do have exceptionally keen senses - and Tyson was obviously aware of the ghostly soldiers. He reacted strongly to their presence and, when they vanished, was ready to resume his interrupted walk as if nothing had happened.

"Time, like an ever-rolling stream, bears all its sons away ...." So says Isaac Watts' old hymn 'O God Our Help in Ages Past'. But is everything borne away? What is Time? Does Time actually exist? Only as a measure of change or decay, says current scientific thinking.

What separates our Past from our Present and Future? Is it possible that on rare occasions we see more than we should, that we break out of our limited 'Now'? Can timeslips or timewarps occur? If so, do we somehow enter a different age or do dimensions occasionally overlap to give us a brief unexpected glimpse of another point in time? So many questions but no real answers, unless Phil's experiences on Brading Down point us some way towards this conundrum.

HAUNTED VILLA

Nestling into the hillside at the foot of Brading Down, is Brading Roman Villa, a Grade 1 listed building and a fine example of a courtyard villa, the type owned by the wealthiest Roman Britons. Occupied for more than three centuries, the Villa was started in about 50AD. Its stone walls, which would probably have been no more than waist-high, supported a stout timber frame, filled with wattle and daub. Inside, the walls were brightly painted.

The Villa's decline started after 400AD, when estates in southern Britain suffered increasing raids by barbarian pirates. Sixty years later, much of the main house seems to have been turned over to farm workshops. Finally, the building was abandoned, anything useful was scavenged and the structure fell into ruin. As centuries passed, the Villa was lost to both sight and memory.

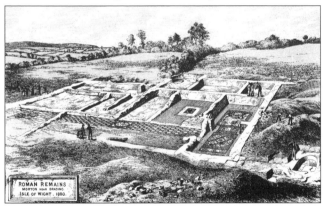

It didn't see the light of day again until 1879 when a keen amateur archaeologist, Captain Thorp of Yarbridge, spent time and energy trying to find the site after children showed him their treasures,

The discovery of Brading Roman Villa, an 1880 engraving

some Roman coins and artefacts from fields at Morton Farm. The farmer, Mr Munns, also became interested and, while making holes for a sheep pen, he struck a mosaic floor. By April 1880, about half of the Villa had been excavated and the remains of walls, fine mosaic pavements and evidence of a sophisticated plumbing and hypocaust system were uncovered.

When it became clear that the rest of the house extended beyond the field and onto the nearby Oglander estate, Louisa, Lady Oglander, bought the whole site so that excavations could continue. Now, as a registered Charity, the Oglander Roman Trust is carrying the story of Brading Roman Villa and its unique mosaics into the new millennium.

A Baby's Bones

The Roman well there was discovered and excavated in 1880 when local labourers explored the shaft to a depth of almost 80 feet. Since then almost six feet of debris has accumulated at the bottom. When this was recently re-excavated with the help of Bradford Pothole Club, more than 15,000 coins, mostly English pennies and half-pennies were discovered. During those dark years of the First century AD, the Villa's rock-cut well also attracted a variety of pagan offerings. Before it was closed, possibly after running dry, even people were thrown in - for human bones were discovered almost 15 feet from the top. In 1880, these were thought to be those of a young man aged between 17 and 20. More recently however, the bones have been re-examined by a forensic pathologist who, in 2004, identified the remains of at least five people in the well, including the bones of a young baby.

An Ancient Shepherd

Former Isle of Wight Police Inspector Neville Carr has long been fascinated by Roman history, so when he retired from the force in the mid 1990s, he was delighted to find a part-time job at the Brading Roman Villa. Ten years on, he's the full-time Curator for the Oglander Roman Trust. He has also helped oversee a major project to protect the fabric of the Villa with a purpose-built cover and highly innovative visitor centre, thanks to a Heritage Lottery Fund grant of £2.7 million.

Is this the ghostly shepherd?

Although he's not met any of the Villa's ghosts himself (and doesn't believe in such things) Neville admits that some shocked visitors have reported seeing the figure of an ancient shepherd dressed in a white smock, who walks

The new purpose-built £2.7 million visitor centre at Brading Roman Villa

through the northwest wall of the Villa. "A lot of people come to me and say they feel some sort of presence in the Villa, particularly in that corner, while others remark on a change in atmosphere in the same area."

It may be significant that one of the Villa's mosaics shows a shepherd wearing a smock. On his head is a Phrygian Cap (worn by emancipated slaves as a symbol of their freedom) and he carries panpipes and a crook – a reminder perhaps that in Roman times, wool from sheep reared on the nearby Downs was an important product.

Some years ago, before animals were prohibited, many dogs refused to approach that corner. Wendy Gannon was mortified when hers, a highly-trained working dog 'went berserk' in the Villa, barking insistently at that corner.

And was it wishful thinking or an echo from the mists of time, when an apparently psychic visitor to Brading Villa told Neville that she had heard the strains of a musical instrument, and seen an elaborate entrance room and the apparition of a Roman lady appear to her?

Why not visit this haunting historical place and see for yourself? Man has used the site since at least 10,000BC, so you might expect it to have accumulated a few ghosts in that time. "However, whether the ghostly shepherd continues to appear in the new building remains to be seen," said Neville with a smile.

ROCK COTTAGE

An old stone cottage at Brighstone seems an unlikely haunt for a ghostly Roman centurion, however its proximity to an old Roman Villa, which was excavated in the 1970s, may throw some light on the haunting. Especially as some of the two-foot square chalk blocks from the Villa were used to build the cottage in 1701.

The Scotcher family bought Old Rock Cottage in the late 1950s. An old blacksmith's cottage and forge, it was in a very dilapidated state with no floors and little in the way of a roof, Martin Scotcher recalls.

Now a McTimoney chiropractor at a Newport therapy centre, Martin, who still owns the cottage, remembers his childhood home as a very 'interesting' place to grow up in. "I was aware from a very young age that it was haunted," he said. "One of my earliest memories is of sitting in my cot upstairs and watching shadows on the floor. I could see my own shadow, that of my teddy bear, and the shadow of another, unseen child in there with us. I still remember screaming loudly when I saw it."

Martin also remembers helping archaeologists with the partial re-excavation work at the Villa across the lane from Old Rock Cottage, between 1974 and 1976, before the site was filled in once more. The old cottage points up the valley in the direction of The Longstone, a Neolithic standing stone which has long been associated with pagan rituals and witchcraft on the Island.

Evidence of the cottage's own pagan past can be found in the form of a stone gargoyle-like, carved head with bulging eyes and a rolled tongue, which the family found on an outer wall and incorporated into the cottage during renovations. Much of the supernatural activity at Old Rock Cottage centres around the rear bedroom downstairs, where the old smithy once stood.

"This part of the house has always felt cooler and in some intangible way, more isolated than the rest," said Martin. "Sometimes in the early hours, often at around 2am, the door, which was the original 300-year-old wooden one, would burst open and lights would go on. Sometimes the television would also be switched on.

"That door would be flung open so violently that you could almost feel the change in pressure. My mother sometimes felt spooked there and refused to go outside the back of the cottage at night. She would also lose small items of jewellery in the cottage – which never turned up again – much to her annoyance."

Old Rock cottage, Brighstone, was built with stone from the Roman Villa across the road and a Roman ghost was seen here

Over the years, some solid-looking apparitions have appeared at Old Rock Cottage, including a lady in old-fashioned rustic style clothing who would sit on the end of the bed. Martin's father Norman, who died in the late 1990s, also saw a ghostly Roman centurion walking through the cottage on more than one occasion. This spirit was always seen coming from the direction of the old villa site and moving south.

"When my father, who was ill with Parkinson's Disease, slept in the back bedroom downstairs, he would sometimes say that he had been woken in the night by ghostly figures sitting on the bed. It was such a regular thing that we hardly took any notice after a while. He would also talk of seeing apparitions outside in Lynch Lane and of hearing a ghostly horse trotting down the lane."

LONGSTONE SACRIFICES

Less than a mile due west of Old Rock Cottage, and in a direct line with it, is The Longstone near Mottistone village, an impressive standing stone, some 15 feet tall. This sandstone megalith and its smaller recumbent companion once formed the entrance to a Neolithic chambered long barrow. The barrow also appears to be aligned to the summer Solstice sunrise.

Tradition asserts that the Druids, Celts and subsequent invaders used the stones for religious purposes - each endowing the site with their own set of beliefs. This site was certainly important to the Romans, who are thought to have used the Longstone as a shrine to the soldiers' cult of the Sun god Mithras, which involved the sacrifice of live bulls.

Mithras was worshipped as a god from around 1400BC until at least 400AD and ancient Mesopotamian tablets make it clear that he was a god of contract and fellowship, closely associated with the Sun. There were seven grades of initiation in this mystery religion, each with a symbolic name; Raven, Bridegroom, Soldier, Lion, Persian, Sun's messenger and finally Father. Candidates also underwent a ceremony in which they suffered a symbolic death and re-birth. Like the other ancient mystery religions, Mithraism maintained strict secrecy about its teachings and practices, revealing them only to initiates. The temples, called mithraea, were usually built underground in imitation of caves, so perhaps at The Longstone, the underground Neolithic chamber was used for this purpose.

There were many hundreds - perhaps thousands - of Mithraic temples in the Roman empire. The greatest concentrations were in Rome itself, and in those places in the empire (often at the most distant frontiers) where Roman soldiers - a major segment of the cult's membership - were stationed.

Roman Mithras had many similarities to Christianity, its greatest rival. Mithras was born of a virgin; remained celibate; his worship involved baptism; the partaking of bread marked with a cross and wine as sacrificial blood; held Sundays sacred and Mithras was 'born' on 25 December. These similarities frightened the early Church leaders and as Christianity became the formal religion of the Roman Empire, the Cult of Mithras came under attack in the fifth century. Temples of Mithras, like most other pagan temples, were destroyed and churches built over them. But The Longstone escaped such a fate. During the Dark Ages the site was a meeting place - 'moteres stan' means the speaker's stone in old English - hence Mottistone. The Saxons used these places to announce judgements and allow debate on important matters. Even today The Longstone is still associated with witchcraft and pagan practices. (Read about this in *Ghosts of the Isle of Wight Book III*)

Chapter Two

WEIRDNESS AT BLACKWATER AND GATCOMBE

PHANTOM TEA FLASK

Did a couple of workmen drink a cup of tea brought to them by a ghost? Incredible as this might seem, it's the only explanation Reg Blake and his mate could think of after their strange experience.

In 1980, they were repairing the roof of the little 80-seat, corrugated iron St Barnabas Church at Blackwater, near Newport. "We had taken the tin sheets off the roof and were re-filling the cavity with sawdust for insulation, when a little, elderly lady in old-fashioned clothes walked in carrying an ancient aluminium Thermos with cup handles which folded back into the flask. She called out to us, ' Hello! I have brought you some tea. I will leave it on the altar. I live just down the road, so you can bring the flask back when you have finished with it'.

"We thanked the old lady and after she had left, we poured ourselves a cup. But it was stone cold and tasted horrible. We couldn't drink it; we just poured it away. When we finished for the day, my mate went to the address the old lady had given us to return the flask. But there was no house there, just an empty plot where a building had once stood."

Puzzled by this, they told the churchwarden the next day when she came to see how work was progressing. When they described the old lady and the address she had given them, the churchwarden smiled and told them, 'That was my predecessor. Sadly she died three years ago'!

Now deconsecrated, the little red-painted tin church has been resurrected as a busy fresh fruit and vegetable shop where, in place of the altar, stand displays of oranges and lemons.

The old tin Church of St Barnabas at Blackwater

Owner Tudor Radcliffe, who bought the building as an empty shell from the Church of England in November 1992, after it was declared surplus to requirements, hasn't been visited by an elderly lady with an old-fashioned Thermos yet. "If she does I won't be drinking the tea!" he said.

GATCOMBE GHOST-GIRL

From time immemorial people everywhere have enjoyed a good ghost story. Tales of the unknown and undead simultaneously attract yet repulse us. Spine-chilling legends of graveyard ghouls are legion – yet in reality, reports of hauntings in churchyards and cemeteries are rare. However, by tradition ghosts and graveyards are inextricably linked, so when a group of friends set out for a spooky adventure one Halloween, they made for the tiny St Olave's Church at Gatcombe.

The church lies at almost the geographical centre of the Island, between two great ley lines that run from the ancient stone circle at Avebury through some of the most important prehistoric sites in southern England. It was built as a manorial chapel in the thirteenth century by the noble Estur family of Gatcombe House.

In the little stone church can be found one of the most important carved oak figures on the Island, an early fourteenth century effigy of a knight with crossed legs, denoting that the Crusader attended his lord in the Holy Land. A small crouched dog lies at his feet; an angel at his pillow. The knight is thought to be Edward Estur who returned from the Crusades in 1365, with head injuries and loss of memory. Around this recumbent figure has been woven a charming tale, the result of a harmless hoax which over time has become an established local legend!

Lucy Lightfoot

The story of Lucy Lightfoot, who left her horse tethered at the gateway to Gatcombe Church when she went inside to shelter from an electrical storm, was first penned by a cheery Welsh cleric, the Reverend James Evans, when he was the Vicar of Gatcombe between 1965 and 1973.

In his imaginative mystery story, young Lucy, who was apparently infatuated with the wooden effigy, vanishes during the combined storm and a total solar eclipse in 1831 to be transported back in time to Cyprus in 1364, where she accompanies her Knight, Edward Estur, to the Crusades.

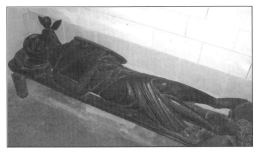

The wooden effigy of Crusader Edward Estur

Reverend Evans wrote:
Time present and time past
Are both then present in time future
And time future becomes contained in time past
'Thus Lucy Lightfoot just stepped lightly into the past and just stayed there, as she always longed, with her loved one. In Gatcombe we still believe that strange and even supernatural events may still occur on this terraqueous globe.'

However, fact often is stranger than fiction and our group of ghost hunters now fervently agrees with the late Reverend Evans that Gatcombe certainly has supernatural links! Events of that night, 31 October 1995, are etched in their memories, and Xavier Baker who now runs Ventnor Brewery, can still hardly believe what happened.

"As it was Halloween several of us went out looking for ghosts in two cars. First of all we went to Knighton Gorges but saw nothing there, so on our way home we called at Gatcombe. Actually we never expected anything to happen - it was all just a bit of a laugh. At Gatcombe Church it was pitch dark but we had a torch to light our way through the graveyard as we walked towards the church. Suddenly we saw a movement near the old stone wall. Shining the torch across the graves we saw a little girl there.

"She had bobbed blonde hair and wore what looked like a pale dress or nightie. She hid behind a gravestone, then ran towards us in a mischievous and playful way, suddenly darting away into the darkness towards the gate. We didn't stay to see any more, we just scarpered!

"At a friend's house in nearby Rookley we talked over what we had seen and agreed to return in daylight to investigate further. By day we felt foolish, telling ourselves we had imagined the whole thing. We even spoke to a gravedigger working there and apologised for larking about the night before.

"We searched the area where the little girl had appeared and looked at the headstone she had hidden behind. What we saw gave us quite a shock. That grave belonged to a child who had died one October, a few years before."

In a strange little postscript to the above story, I was also contacted by Newport teenager Alice Taylor, who wrote: "I experienced a bone-chilling visit to Gatcombe Church one day when I went there with my mother. The moment we drove up the path shivers struck my neck. Walking through the rickety gates made my spine shake, and I was pushed by some unseen force towards a young girl's grave. Do you know anything of this place being inhabited by a lost soul, especially if it was a young girl?"

THE DOG WHO DANCES

Another legend associated with Gatcombe Church, which has become part of Island folklore, thanks to the Reverend Evans, is that of Flacon Caprice, the little dog which rests at the feet of Crusader Edward Estur. According to a professor of Mediaevalism and Symbolic Rites, the animal is a totemistic creature, which is believed by occultists to come to life on Midsummer night (June 24).

The legend tells that 'When moonlight envelops the church, the pathway becomes lit with an unearthly radiance, a strange greenish light makes a circle in the centre of the pathway leading to the church and forms a track into the woods. Then the little wooden dog, Flacon Caprice, awakes from his deathlike sleep and dances on his hind legs in the green centre of light. And as he dances, along the track come the little folk that dwell in the hollow hills around Chillerton Downs, to dance with him until the church belfry owl hoots at midnight. Then Flacon Caprice tells stories of his adventures to his fairy friends until dawn when they all return to their own worlds.' This strange event is said to happen only once or twice every hundred years. So, as they say, don't hold your breath....

A DARK FIGURE

When they noticed a man waiting in the bus shelter at the side of the road, one dark, very wet night, Martin Holbrook and his two friends decided to stop and offer him a lift. It was the early 1980s and Martin, then a teenager, and his companions, Simon Timms and Raymond Attrill, were on their way to the cinema in Newport.

"It was a filthy night; pitch dark and pouring with rain," recalled Martin. "As we turned out of the lane from Gatcombe onto the main road, our headlights picked out the figure of a man waiting in the old wooden bus shelter at the side of the road. He was dressed in what looked like a long trench coat and a hat.

"Ray slowed down and said, 'Let's stop and give him a lift.' So we stopped the car and reversed back to the shelter. But it was empty. The figure had vanished. Was it a ghost? I don't know. But we had all seen him, waiting there in the dark."

St Olave's Church at Gatcombe where a young ghost-girl was seen one Halloween

This photograph shows numbers 7 and 8 Holyrood Street in the early 20th century

Chapter Three

HAUNTINGS IN HOLYROOD STREET

The town of Newport is almost 900 years old, although there's evidence of occupation by the Romans and of even earlier settlement by Bronze Age people some 4,500 years ago. Over the centuries Newport has been sacked and burned by French invaders, its population decimated by outbreaks of plague. Despite this, the Island's main market town and busy port has survived and prospered. In recent years the pace of change has accelerated. Gone are many small, family-run shops and businesses, torn down to make way for new supermarkets and car parks. But those who know where to look can still discover parts of old Newport, which those long-dead townsfolk would still recognise.

Many ghosts linger here, particularly in the area of Holirodestret (today's Holyrood Street). One of the oldest parts of Newport, ancient deeds show that in 1643 there were at least three small breweries operating here, alongside the town's workhouse. When the Island's House of Industry was built at Parkhurst, the old workhouse became a Bridewell or prison where until 1901, 'incorrigible offenders' were gaoled for crimes like poaching, smuggling and drunkenness.

After it was demolished, the site was incorporated into the huge Mew Langton's Royal Brewery complex. This in turn ceased production after more than 300 years of brewing beer for pubs and alehouses, as well as supplying the Army at home and as far afield as China and India. Following a devastating fire in the late 1970s, an award-winning sheltered housing complex was built in its place. Here, in January 2003, the ghost of a Victorian lady in a white lace bonnet was seen by a startled elderly resident of Brewery Court, who awoke one night and caught sight of the woman's figure leaning over her bed.

To the north of Holyrood Street was the town's railway station, while nearby was an establishment known simply as 'The Theatre', which opened in 1786. Patronised by the cream of Newport society, in 1832 a ticket for a box cost three shillings (15p). Nearby, between 1760 and 1820, the local gentry met for suppers and dancing in the ballroom and assembly rooms above the Sun Inn, where dancing usually continued well into the early hours. Members of this exclusive set met monthly when the moon was full – so that they could travel home by moonlight.

This Primitive Methodist Chapel has been incorporated into the premises of Hurst's

In 1839 a Primitive Methodist Chapel was built nearby and to this day, parts of the original structure can be seen within Hurst's shop, whose premises have expanded to occupy a considerable part of Holyrood Street. Today Hurst's is one of the oldest-established businesses in the town. William Hurst, founder of Wheeler & Hurst, iron and brass founders, died in 1927, after living most of his life in the haunted Rock Cottage in Castle Road. (Read the story in Chapter 11)

SPIRITS HAVING FLOWN

The Sun Inn, which stood on the corner of Holyrood Street and Lugley Street, was the scene of a dark and violent tragedy which ended in a double murder almost three centuries ago. The historic inn closed in 1976, but ghostly echoes of those long-forgotten murders, involving Francesca, a young serving girl; Ralph, a stable boy who befriended her; and the Pigman, a local ruffian who murdered Ralph; still resonated there. (Read their sinister story in *More Ghosts of the Isle of Wight*)

A Little Leather Shoe

Graham Morris who bought the old coaching inn made a gruesome discovery in a tiny attic room. Hidden behind a chimney was a dusty bundle containing a bloodstained nightgown and a bag of ancient leather shoes, which featured in the story of Francesca and Ralph. More recently, another little leather shoe was found in the building, this time concealed under floorboards on the first floor. During renovation works, carpenter and joiner Colin Hansford discovered this child's tiny shoe - containing of all things, a walnut shell - which had been placed there many, many years earlier. (see photograph opposite)

For centuries, shoes were hidden in buildings to protect occupants against witchcraft and evil spirits. These shoes are found in 'spiritual middens' inside walls, up chimneys, under floorboards, or anywhere else evil spirits could enter the home. Most of the shoes are worn, many belonged to children and only rarely are pairs ever found. Shoes were

expensive items, so they were repaired again and again until they fell apart. As a result, the shoe was a unique item, perfectly fitting only the wearer.

If the tiny shoe was intended to ward off restless spirits at the old Sun Inn, the charm

The child's shoe and walnut from the old Sun Inn

clearly failed to work. It took a very different kind of ritual to clear the building of its resident ghosts.

In a poignant postscript to this haunting, Glenn Creed, a partner at the Watchbell House complementary therapy centre in Lugley Street, opposite the former inn, witnessed a remarkable 'psychic cleansing' there, late one summer afternoon in 2001. At the time, Benedict's Wine Merchants and Delicatessen occupied the premises, and manager Lynne Holland mentioned to Glenn that the shop was still haunted.

"I was never scared there," Lynne said. "Although I would often have to lock up at night in the dark. But it was an odd place; at night things would fall off the shelves for no reason. This happened a lot. One day as I was serving, a box full of glasses came crashing off a shelf and shattered on the floor. There was certainly a presence there and one of the staff, a young Thai girl, actually left because she felt someone was behind her all the time."

Glenn explained, "A mainland psychic was conducting a workshop at Watchbell House at the time, and when I told her of the haunted Sun Inn, she offered her help. Late that afternoon we went across the road and the psychic 'tuned in'. She told us there were at least three spirits in the building; a young girl, a young man and an older man. They were unwilling to leave, as the girl, Francesca, was 'keeping' the others there in some way.

"So the psychic asked her spirit guides to help. They apparently rounded up these earthbound souls and persuaded them to move 'towards the light'. I admit I was quite sceptical and stood in the

The old haunted Sun Inn in Holyrood Street

doorway chatting with Lynne, as this was going on," admitted Glenn. "I didn't believe anything was going to happen - and certainly not immediately," he added. "Suddenly I felt a whoosh of charged energy like a breath of light, fresh air, rushing through me. This was followed a couple of seconds later by a slower, dense, heavy sensation which passed right through me as I stood in the doorway. As I felt it, the psychic turned to us and announced, 'They've gone.'

"I retorted, 'I know, I felt them pass right through me!' By this time I was starting to feel nauseous. That second, heavy force had been stale and cloying, I felt like I was wading through treacle. It took much longer to move through me than that, bright energy which zipped through first. Lynne, however, just felt a rush of freezing cold air pass through her, which she found surprising on such a hot summer's day.

"I told my psychic friend what had happened. By this time I was feeling quite ill and was unwell for several hours; I was sick and lethargic. She told me to rest and to drink plenty of water. Apart from this unpleasant side effect, it was an amazing experience, which I wouldn't have missed for the world. The difference between those two energies was incredible," said Glenn.

And since that time, the old Sun Inn premises have felt 'different' too. Lynne noticed that the atmosphere instantly lightened and much of the ghostly activity stopped. After Benedict's closed, the Andrew Ross Hair Salon opened in the corner premises. Staff report that odd noises and footsteps can still be heard, but they trouble no one.

A WISTFUL SOUL

Elsewhere in this part of the town a remarkable number of old buildings are haunted. In the late 1970s and early 1980s, writer and former postman Mike Acton would often stay in a friend's flat at

Holyrood Street, above what is now Mike Heath Antiques. Years ago the building was an old-fashioned confectioners and sweet shop run by Miss Gladys Ashby, a well-liked local character.

Whenever Mike stayed overnight he used the bedroom at the rear, overlooking the back yard while his friend, Ray Lee, would sleep in the front room.

Mike recalls, "One night in the middle of summer I was in bed reading when I felt the temperature drop very suddenly. At the time I was facing the wall because the bedroom light was poor and this was the best position to catch the light. Suddenly my whole body seemed to be paralysed. I managed to turn at last and saw that over by the doorway, the solid-looking figure of a woman was peering in my direction. She was dressed in black, old-fashioned clothing and wore a shawl around her shoulders.

"She seemed to be trying to speak, but made no sound," said Mike. "She had a very pale face, pinched in a wistful expression, and I think she was somewhere in her mid-thirties. She wasn't a frightening apparition, but she gave off an overwhelming feeling of sadness as she slowly faded from sight a few seconds later. This sadness was quite overwhelming and even after she had vanished, the coldness remained for some time."

Mike frequently stayed in that flat, but never saw her again, although he sometimes had a sense of being watched and would often get a cold feeling in that bedroom. "This has haunted me since then. I would love to know who the woman was and especially why she was so very sad."

Although the Heath family, who opened an antiques shop there in 1981, have never seen the mournful spirit, they have heard ghostly voices and the sound of footsteps on the stairs. As teenagers, sisters Frances and Emily were watching television with friends in the first floor living room at the rear of the building, when they heard footsteps walking upstairs from the shop -

A woman's sad ghost was seen here

which was locked and secure. They hurried to the top of the stairs to see who was there, but the staircase was empty. Aby, a friend who stayed the night, wondered the next morning who had been walking around downstairs in the early hours. Nobody had.

"We often hear the sound of muffled voices in the living room, as if the television is on. It's like a blurred conversation - you can never make out the actual words. We feel a presence but nothing has ever appeared. One night when my dad was sleeping in the front bedroom, he felt the duvet being pulled off him. He doesn't believe in ghosts, but he can't explain that!

"It can't be coincidence that the woman's ghost appeared in that back bedroom, which is now the living room where we hear those voices," said Frances, who confessed to using a Ouija board there on several occasions. "It's not something I do any more," she added. "You never know what you are in touch with."

FESTOONED IN DARK COBWEBS

Years ago a huddle of tumbledown houses nearby was swept away to make room for a private car park. Access to this little slum, which was known as Flux's Court, was through a narrow alleyway next to 7 Holyrood Street.

In 1979 John and Ann Langley opened a health food shop at 7 and 8 Holyrood Street, which they called 'Grain of Truth'. A woman's ghost wearing an old-fashioned wrap-around floral print 'pinny' haunted this two-storey building, which dates back to the 1700s.

Records show that in the 1870s, Job, William and Richard Wightman worked as 'umbrella makers, repairers and chimney sweepers' at No 7, while No 8 was the workshop for cabinet-maker and upholsterer Mr Burton. By the turn of the new century, the premises had become George Bricknell's grocery shop, run by two tiny, elderly sisters who, John was told, were so short they were unable to reach the thick cobwebs which hung festooned in dark corners of the shop. It's also known that four female members of the family died in the building.

"When we took the place on it was in a dreadful state," said Ann. "The shop still had old-fashioned gas lamps and there was no electricity upstairs. We had to completely rewire and refit it, but while John was working there on his own, something kept 'borrowing' his tools."

John added, "There was no feeling of malice at all, it was more like practical jokes, as if the presence was doing whatever it could to attract my attention. At first I was camping out there in the totally empty property when I started to lose my tools. I was only using pliers, cutters and a screwdriver, but every so often when I put one of them down, it would disappear!

"I would place it on the floor by my side and when I reached for it again, it wasn't there. I searched high and low, but a few minutes later the missing tool would be returned. After a while I cottoned on to what was happening and, speaking to what I thought must be the invisible practical joker, I said, 'Come on, a joke's a joke. I can't see you, but I know you are there. Now leave my tools alone!'

"When I took the floorboards up I found an old green-handled screwdriver there and I added it to my collection of tools, but this, too, would go missing and I would always find it back under the floorboards again. Eventually I gave up and just left it there."

One evening when John was standing at the large kitchen window facing the rear yard, he saw a visitor walking past the window towards the back door. "It was a little old lady wearing a wrap-around print pinafore. When I opened the door however, she had completely vanished. I had seen a ghost.

"Our daughters, Donna and Andrea, are quite sensitive and when we moved into Holyrood Street, they sensed a presence there from the outset. Andrea heard a woman's footsteps coming up the empty stairs, and all the time we lived there - for almost seven years - Basil, the family cat, was permanently spooked. He literally lived on his nerves and would leap into the air for no apparent reason. His fur and tail would bristle and he would often stare intently at an unseen presence. It wasn't until we moved out in 1986 to live on a narrow boat, that Basil settled down again," John laughed.

SPIRIT OF THE SILK ROAD

When former BT engineer and oriental art dealer Mike Nolan bought the premises from John and Ann, he opened Silk Road, a shop specialising in imported Asian gifts, pictures and handicrafts. Now he and his wife, Mem, plan to open a Thai restaurant on the ground floor. Mike has never seen the ghost there, although he found the rear of the building to be unnaturally cold when he first moved in and friends also commented on the penetrating chill there. Since their children were born, however, all such feelings have been swept away in the hustle and bustle of family life.

There was however, one odd little occurrence a few years ago, when their daughter, Maya, was a baby. Mem woke in the middle of the night to hear her chattering and giggling to herself in the adjoining room. When she went in to check, she found Maya lying in her cot, gazing fixedly at a spot near the ceiling. She was laughing and waving her tiny hands about in such delight that she didn't even look round when her mother spoke to her, so focussed was she on that invisible visitor – a tiny, but kindly elderly lady, perhaps?

A TROUBLED GHOST

While the Langley family ran Grain of Truth, they were aware that a troublesome spirit also bothered a neighbouring business at 14/15 Holyrood Street, the old-established printing firm of Yelf Brothers.

John recalls, "There was a very strong presence there which was thought to be a poltergeist. At night when the place was locked, papers and printing jobs were thrown around. When staff arrived for work in the morning, they would find them strewn about the floor. I believe things got so bad that a local psychic was called in to sort things out," said John. "When she made contact with the ghost she discovered the building was haunted by the spirit of a former owner who was troubled by talk of selling or closing the business. This was his way of registering his displeasure."

Sadly that ghostly premonition was all too correct. This old family business, founded in 1816 by former grocer William Yelf, a respected businessman and Methodist superintendent, has now closed. His grandson, William Richard Yelf, passed away there in 1896, in the very house where he was born in 1825. Did his agitated spirit warn of the impending closure? Or could the troubled ghost have been old William's own son?

For William Wheeler Yelf, that son, was certainly not the pillar of the community he appeared to be. In 1853, in his capacity as secretary to the Isle of Wight Savings Bank, he appeared at the Winchester Assizes facing charges of fraud and embezzlement. He pleaded guilty to defrauding the bank of £4,182 over ten years – although, with interest, the books showed the discrepancy to be double that. A broken man, his health in ruins, Yelf was sentenced to transportation for life. But the sentence was never carried out. He died of bronchitis and heart disease while awaiting the convict ship bound for Australia.

The old building, with its flagstone floors and quaint rear courtyard is now a pine furniture showroom, where proprietor, Simon Harris, reports that the ghost has now gone and all is quiet on the supernatural front.

The old premises of Yelf's printers

A MISCHIEVOUS SPIRIT

As Merlin's Return and the Rowan Tree Centre, a New Age shop and complementary therapies centre, 14 Holyrood Street has seen an ironic about-turn since it served as an Army recruiting office in the pre-war days of the 1930s.

Karen Way and Sue Cheek, who run the business, have been aware of a ghostly child, called Elspeth or Elizabeth, who plays at the top of the stairs near the attics. "She is a mischievous spirit, for some mornings we have come in to find things such as tarot cards and candles have been thrown onto the floor in the night," said Karen. One day, Sue was coming down those stairs when she suddenly found herself at the bottom. She is certain she was pushed, and has an idea that it was a small ghostly hand that did the pushing! A large black ghost-cat has also been seen around the shop and back rooms. An elderly neighbour confirms that years ago, such an animal lived there with previous owners.

IMPISH GHOST AT SEAL HOUSE

Adjoining Holirodestret in centuries past was Shispoole Street (today's Sea Street) where local merchants built their warehouses. Some, which were exempt from paying wharfage dues, were known as 'Free Stores'. Here, too, over the centuries, near the busy port, an incredible

A little grinning ghost was seen at Seal House

number of inns and beer houses such as the Dolphin, Fountain, Banner, Anchor, Castle View, Packhorse, and Queen Charlotte sprang up, among the free stores and merchants' houses.

Seal House in Sea Street is a large three-storey house, built in the late seventeenth century, which overlooks Newport Quay. One of the few remaining examples of a wealthy merchant's house, with wood-panelled rooms and extensive brick-lined cellars, it is home to Andrew Turner, who became the Island's MP in June 2001, and his partner, Carole.

However, evidence of a more chequered history can still be seen above its door, where an advertisement discovered during restoration work in 1991 reads, "Frederick King. Licensed to sell beer by Retail to be drunk on the premises." As 'The Sloop', it was briefly a Victorian beer house, before becoming home to one of the Shepard brothers, who ran a major carriers and removal business in Quay Street.

Seal House is haunted by a little grinning red-haired apparition, which has been seen kneeling at the end of a bed. This ghost made such an impression on young Joy Adsett, that almost half-a-century later she could still picture him clearly. Joy, whose family was renting Seal House at the time recalled, "I could only have been about five years old, and when I saw that face appear at the end of the bed, I screamed for my mum and dad. They rushed upstairs, but the apparition with the impish grin just faded away and I never saw him again," said Joy.

Although neither Andrew nor Carole has yet seen the little grinning ghost, they are keeping a wary eye on the end of the bed …

Chapter Four

THE DARK SIDE OF VENTNOR

THE EGG AND BACON MAN

A ghost known locally as the 'egg and bacon man' still haunts the old RAF base in Upper Ventnor where he was stationed as a cook at the barracks. Still wearing his uniform, with a short jacket, dark green socks and heavy boots, this wartime apparition is in his thirties and clean-shaven with short, dark hair. He doesn't appear solid, which is probably just as well, for he tends to walk through walls. Instead he resembles a reflection as he moves about Wendy and Gary Lacey's home.

Their bungalow, which was built in the early 1990s, clearly poses no obstacle to the egg and bacon man's ghost, for he wanders around at will in his own dimension, gliding through walls and furniture. To the Laceys it's just 'one of those things'.

"We might not see him for a few months, then we'll smell bacon cooking and he appears again, wandering about the place any time of the day or night having his phantom fry-up," said Wendy. "He was around quite frequently at the time of the 60th anniversary of the Battle of Britain in the summer of 2000."

Only once has the presence of the ghostly cook caused any trouble. Wendy was sitting alone in the lounge one evening, when she felt a sudden, excruciating pain on her arm. "I shouted, 'Gary, someone's bitten me'. I looked down to see a great big bite mark on my left forearm. We could actually see indentations left by the teeth. They were there for three or four days. I had a bruise come up which really hurt.

"I was shocked and indignant. Although I had not seen him, I knew it was the ghost that had bitten me. I had a good moan at him and told him to clear off if he was going to be so horrible! He never did it again."

This is an unusually tolerant attitude, you might think, but Wendy is not easily frightened by the unexplained. Her grandmother ran a Spiritualist Church and it seems Wendy has inherited her talent for seeing the world of spirits. "His other annoying habit is to take things, usually paperwork, which disappear for days or weeks at a time. They usually turn up in unlikely places, such as inside a pillow or the pocket of a suit which hasn't been worn for years. Recently I spent most of the day searching for two invoices which had vanished," she complained.

The ghostly soldier is usually glimpsed in the kitchen, lounge or dining room. "We were sitting with our son having dinner the other day and all three of us saw him. We think there's a ghost-cat here too. It has been seen disappearing around corners in the house – attracted by the smell of cooking bacon no doubt!"

The bungalow in Hazel Close was built on land once occupied by the concrete prefabricated barracks of the Upper Ventnor RAF base. Servicemen working at the top-secret wartime radar station on St Boniface Down were stationed there from the late 1930s onwards, and Wendy believes that the unfortunate cook was killed during a heavy bombing raid.

For years after the war, the old camp lay empty. The land later formed part of the Transatlantic Plastics factory site before being developed for housing. Traces of the camp have long since vanished, although the remains of the nearby radar station can still be seen on top of St Boniface Down, the Island's highest point.

The radar towers can be seen in this photograph of Ventnor taken in the 1950s

CHRISTMAS GHOSTS

As a mother herself, Wendy Lacey (who provided the previous story) still worries about the fate of two little girls whose pathetically pale, bruised and neglected ghosts appeared at the foot of her bed one night.

In the early 1980s, she and her husband and their young son Robert, were living in the upper two floors of a four-storey house in North Street at Ventnor. The first warning of something strange there came when

Wendy's elder brother, a frequent visitor, refused to use their bathroom, preferring instead to go downstairs to the other flat. "He would never explain why and it became a bit of a family joke," said Wendy.

As a toddler, young Robert hated going to sleep in his bedroom and also refused to use the bathroom at night. Wendy would sometimes go in there to find the taps turned on and the toilet flushing when she was alone in the flat.

The mystery deepened when one night, she was woken by the sensation of someone pushing against her feet. Thinking it was her son she sat up and opened her eyes. There at the end of the bed stood two little girls, aged about eight and ten. Both were stark naked, filthy dirty and smelled simply awful. Wendy could see their pale flesh was horribly bruised, the livid weals clearly visible on thin arms and legs, shoulders and chests. Both girls looked underfed and ill. Suddenly, they spoke, "Wendy, get up. We are here to see you." Shocked, Wendy grabbed at her husband and hissed at him to wake up. He however, wouldn't open his eyes and pulled the covers over his face. The little ghost-girls vanished.

Overcome by what she had just seen, Wendy went downstairs and made herself a pot of tea. The next day she told her brother what had happened; he just nodded and said, "That's why I won't use the toilet in your flat."

He had often sensed he was being watched there, he told Wendy, and had actually seen one of the girls standing in the bath; the other walking down the stairs. Fortunately, both had been dressed, albeit in dirty, ragged clothes, when he encountered them. When Wendy told her friend next door what was happening, the neighbour revealed that the previous owner had spoken of similar happenings.

Other visitors were equally reluctant to use that bathroom, and Wendy confessed that when showering she never closed the curtains around the bath. "It felt too horrid in there," she said with a shudder.

It was some months later, just before Christmas, when she encountered the ghostly children again. Wendy didn't recognise them at first. "The front door bell rang and I went to open it. Standing there in the light from the hall I could see two girls who I think were sisters, dressed in beautiful purple Victorian costumes. Both children were holding little glass lanterns containing candles. They wore crinoline frocks with velvet capes. Their dark hair was curled in long ringlets, decorated with purple ribbons. I was gobsmacked that they had gone to so much trouble, dressing up like that to go carol singing."

In Sweet Voices they Sang

In sweet voices they sang, 'We wish you a Merry Christmas' then stopped and looked expectantly at Wendy. She said, 'Your mother must be so proud of you. You look lovely. Wait there.' Then she ran upstairs to fetch some money for them.

"The girls had with them an old-fashioned glass jamjar on a piece of ribbon, which I tried to put some coins into. But the money wouldn't go in properly. It kept falling through the jamjar. I even held onto the jar and tried to put the money in, but still it ended up on the ground. Finally I took hold of one of the girls' hands and pressed the money into it. Then I wished them both a 'Happy Christmas' and off they went."

It wasn't until Wendy had sat down again that the strangeness of the encounter hit her. "It was surreal. I couldn't believe what had just happened. I immediately went next door to ask my neighbours if the girls had called there. They hadn't." Wendy went to five more houses nearby, but nobody else had seen them. It seemed that her house was the only one they had visited.

"Afterwards I realised they were the same girls I had seen that night in my bedroom, but they were obviously well cared for and younger than when I first saw them. Although I never set eyes on them again, it has haunted me ever since, wondering what on earth happened to turn them from two, beautifully-clothed, cherished children, into those neglected, filthy and abused little waifs."

Although she only saw the girls on two occasions, Wendy now believes that her young son Robert made friends with one of them. For as soon as he was old enough to talk, Robert started chattering to an unseen companion, a little girl he called 'Ju Ju'. He told Wendy that 'Ju Ju' was with him all the time, and even insisted on having a place laid for her at the table next to him. "When we sold the house and moved away he was inconsolable. He sobbed his heart out," Wendy recalled.

When she attempted to research the history of her property, Wendy discovered it was once a Victorian holiday villa, part of the Lansdown Estate. That top floor where the girls appeared had once been the nursery where the resident nanny lived. Sadly, no further information was available. Since Wendy sold the house in 1985, it has had several owners. While visiting a friend who lived opposite her old home, recently, Wendy saw a removal van outside and asked why the latest occupants were leaving. "A little bit of trouble with the girls", replied her friend, knowingly.

A DEAD MAN

When Amanda Davies spent a holiday on the Island with her parents and four-year-old niece, Angharad, in September 2003, the little girl had a curious encounter with a 'dead man' in Ventnor.

Amanda explained, "We stopped off at Ventnor one Monday afternoon and were looking in the window of an antiques/junk shop. It was actually closed and up for sale, due to ill health of the owner. My mother read out a notice on the window explaining this. My niece, who stood in the doorway looking through the glass door, asked, 'Why is there a dead man in there?' Mum, thinking she was asking about the shop owner and the notice, told her the man wasn't dead. He was just ill, she explained.

"However, Angharad turned to Mum and said, ' No, I mean the dead man at the back of the shop. He's holding something. Oh it's a book'. She was pointing towards a bookcase full of old books. I had a really long look, but could see no one there.

"On the way back to the car my niece stopped again, this time to show my father who thought she was making it up. She said to Dad, 'Look Bampi, there he is. I'm not lying, look. He's dropped something. He's bending over. It was the book, now he's looking at us and waving.'

"At this she began to wave back. This completely spooked my parents and we left abruptly. We did not return to Ventnor. I did not get the name of the antiques/junk shop but it was opposite the car park in the centre of the town. My little niece was quite certain she saw what she called the 'dead man' and I thought these were strange words for a four-year-old to use if she was making it up!" said Amanda.

THE PHANTOM NURSE

The elderly lady from Gills Cliff Road, Ventnor, who gave me this next story about the haunted site of the old Royal National Hospital, has asked me not to use her name, but despite this, it is an interesting addition to other accounts of ghosts seen there. You can read the many stories of the haunted hospital in other *Ghosts of the Isle of Wight* books.

It was late in the afternoon of 23 May 1997, and four generations of a Ventnor family; this lady, her daughter, granddaughter and husband with their baby, were leaving Ventnor Botanic Gardens after spending a pleasant hour in warm sunshine in the children's play area.

"Upon leaving we all noticed a figure standing in the car park. It was a very tall lady, all in white, and she was absolutely motionless. Suddenly, I noticed how cold it had become. The lady seemed to be wearing some kind of uniform with a long white or oatmeal skirt, a pale grey blouse and full-length white apron. On her head was a hat with a very large kind of hood over it, which made her head and shoulders look very square. My daughter, jokingly said, 'Oh look, there's a ghost,' which made us peer more closely at her, because she did look oddly out of place. However, we assumed she was possibly in costume for a play or something.

"We climbed into the car and as we drove past her, I glanced back. What struck me was the colour of her face. It resembled grey or blue Plasticine, and she had no expression at all. I clearly saw her nose and mouth, although her eyes just looked like an impression. I also glimpsed her left arm. Her hand had long, slim fingers, which were also this strange grey/blue colour. As I could only see part of her arm I think she must have had three-quarter length sleeves. She was absolutely motionless, like a statue. It only struck me later that it really was a ghost we had seen and I was quite annoyed to think that although we had a camera with us, we did not think to use it! Could this have been the ghost of a nurse from the old hospital?"

A phantom nurse in uniform was seen at Ventnor Botanic Gardens

Chapter Five

MYSTERIOUS TALES OF RYDE

A CHURCH GHOST

Visitors to Ryde may notice a small, tranquil garden just off the top of Union Street. What most won't realise is that this was once the graveyard for the town's oldest church, consecrated as a chapel in 1719 and re-built in 1827. Until that time, pious townsfolk made the twelve-mile round trip each Sunday to their parish church at Newchurch.

The Gothic-style St Thomas' Church is now a Grade II listed building in Ryde's Conservation Area. Sadly neglected over recent years, despite a brief resurgence as a heritage centre for convict transportation records at the time of the Australian bi-centennial, it has now been restored. Thanks to much hard work and generous grants, it is being handed over to the Isle of Wight Council for use as a centre for exhibitions, concerts, meetings and other community-led programmes.

One of the most passionate campaigners for the restoration project has been Ian Smith who, until he retired in 2003, was responsible for conservation and listed buildings with the Island's unitary authority. Ian knows the building well and was a key-holder during the extensive renovation works. However, it was a responsibility he would gladly have relinquished, for over a period of three weeks in March 2002, the intruder alarm went off at 5.30am every Sunday morning. Ian, who lives nearby in Ratcliffe Avenue, was called out by local police to deal with it each time.

He recalled, "The first time it happened I went down and checked it thoroughly. The church was empty, so I reset the alarm and left. The following Sunday the alarm went off again, and once more I was called out. This time I actually felt uneasy in the empty building, particularly in the northeast corner, where the old organ used to be. However, I could find no sign of any intruder, so I reset the alarm and left.

"The third time it happened, my daughter Sharon was home for the weekend. Almost on the dot of 5.30am came the phone call from the police. Sharon offered to come with me, so we drove down to the old church together. When we arrived, the alarm was still ringing, much to the annoyance of neighbours! I shut it off immediately and in the silence

St Thomas' Church at Ryde, in an early engraving

that followed, we both heard the sound of a man's footsteps on the wooden floor of the upper gallery....

"The footsteps were slowly walking towards us from the north-east of the church. We moved quickly into the auditorium, half expecting to see someone running away. We could still hear steps walking to and fro upstairs, so Sharon ran round the outside of the church to check the other door. I stayed in the church. As she returned, the footsteps grew louder and faster. We both checked upstairs, but the area where the sound was coming from was completely empty.

"Suddenly everything went quiet. From the time we arrived to that moment of silence we had heard those footsteps for almost 15 minutes. We both felt quite uncomfortable as we again searched the empty building from top to bottom. Nothing had been disturbed or taken. No doors were open. It's still inexplicable. Those footsteps were so real and we both clearly heard them moving around the gallery in the area where the organ, donated by Miss Mary Brigstocke in 1877, used to stand. Someone or something was definitely walking about up there."

The following Sunday, Ian was awake and ready for that 5.30am call from the police. It never came! "I have been in that church at all sorts of odd hours since then and never once have I heard those footsteps again. In the course of my work I have probably visited thousands of old and historic buildings - many on the Isle of Wight - and never seen a ghost. But now I keep an open mind on the supernatural," he said.

Mystery in the Vault

Who or what set off that alarm and paced the gallery floor in the empty church remains a mystery. The Manor of Ryde was originally owned by the Dillington family of (haunted) Knighton Gorges, and sold to the Player family who oversaw the town's development from a

Ghostly footsteps were heard here in the deconsecrated St Thomas' Church

humble fishing village to a fashionable resort. It's known that the first St Thomas' Chapel was built by Thomas Player in 1719, and when this humble house of worship was unable to accommodate the growing number of worshippers, it was replaced with a modern Gothic building, funded by George Player.

The church later passed, through marriage, to the ownership of the Brigstocke family, several members of whom lie in the vault beneath the east end of the chapel. They maintained the old building until 1956, when George Robert Brigstocke, Lord of the Manor of Ashey and Ryde, died. Services continued there until June 1959, when the doors closed for the last time. From then on, time stood still for the little church.

As Jack Wheeler writes in his informative history of St Thomas' Church, 'The closure in 1959 heralded the darkest period in its history. Its future uncertain, neglect and vandalism seemed to pave the way to ultimate demolition. In the space of a few years, the old building, its walls almost hidden by a thick mantle of ivy, its churchyard overgrown, presented a most forlorn appearance. Surely no House of God has suffered so much in modern times. The vandal found ready access and wantonly destroyed as he went his way. Several unsuccessful attempts were made, by smashing stone flagging and other areas of the floor, to gain access to the vaults below in the search for plunder.'

Some of Ryde's most eminent citizens, including members of the Player and Brigstocke families, lie interred here in the vaulted brick crypt under the church. And here, local legend has it, four of the lead-lined coffins are said to 'move around'. Could it be that these long-dead inhabitants are unhappy that the church is now deconsecrated and no longer a place of worship for the townsfolk of Ryde. Could this be the answer to those mysterious footsteps?

GHOST PARTY AT BRIGSTOCKE

Early in the nineteenth century as Ryde grew in fashion, population and stature, a handsome terrace of ten four-storey houses was built just below St Thomas' Church. Designed by James Sanderson who was also architect for the church and nearby Town Hall, it was known simply as 'The Terrace'. Consisting of uniform large and elegant houses, with a beautiful lawn-like field sloping to the sea, adorned with magnificent oaks and elms, residents included nobility and gentry; the very cream of Ryde society.

Over a century later Brigstocke Terrace, as it is known today, fell into decline. But its fortunes reversed yet again in the 1970s, when local developer Arthur Ellis, gutted, renovated and restored the imposing Georgian terrace to its former splendour - this time as modernised one and two-bedroom apartments.

But the work evidently disturbed a few of the ghosts from The Terrace's elegant past. Builder Kevin Burch of Vectis Road, East Cowes, recalled, "It must have been 1973 when I was working there in Block Five or Six. The building was almost gutted; an empty shell. We had taken out the floors leaving just the joists in place and you could see right up through the building. Suddenly we could hear voices, a sort of loud murmur with laughter and chatter, footsteps, and the chink of glasses. It was the sound of a party

Brigstocke Terrace before its renovation in the 1970s

and it was taking place right above us …"

They looked up at the sky. Of course there was nothing to see, just an empty space where the spirits of Ryde's long dead gentry continue to socialise. And on another occasion Kevin was working alone in Block 10, when he heard the sound of footsteps coming up the stairs. Although no one was there, the sound continued past him and those footsteps went on upwards.…

PATHETIC SHADE

One of Ryde's oldest-known ghosts is said to be the pathetic shade of little Jane, who drowned in a boating accident in 1885 while she was helping her fisherman father. Over the years many people have been puzzled to see a pale, blonde-haired child, limping slowly and painfully along the Esplanade late at night. The girl who has an injured foot, is nearly naked and when she is approached or spoken to by worried passers-by, she disappears into thin air.

Her father apparently survived the accident, but shattered by the tragedy, his mind became unhinged and for years he, too, wandered the seafront in a vain attempt to find his lost daughter. He evidently found peace in death however, for his spirit has not returned.

THE CHURCH STEPS IN

When they moved into their brand new home in a housing development on the outskirts of Ryde, in October 1992, the Andrews family never imagined that it came complete with ghosts. In the six years they lived there, before moving to Haylands, Sally, Steven and their young sons became so concerned at the rising levels of paranormal activity that they finally called in a local priest.

"We were among the first to move in to the estate and everything was fine - at first," recalled Sally. "But soon afterwards we would be sitting in the lounge and hear noises coming from the bedroom above. Every night, between 8pm and 8.30pm, the floorboards would creak as though someone was walking overhead; one of us would rush upstairs to check whether the children were out of bed. They never were. Our old dog would sit and stare at the ceiling, growling. Often we heard a crash, which sounded like a wardrobe falling over. Again we would rush upstairs, only to find nothing out of place. Smells of cigarette smoke would sometimes waft around the lounge – although no one smoked, and annoyingly, small objects such as coins, keys and rings would often disappear for days on end.

"Any time of the day I could be in the kitchen and see a shadow walk past the window. I would wait for the doorbell, but no one ever came," said Sally. Steven, who was then a mobile mechanic, was working in the car park one day when he noticed a man in a trilby hat, with his hands in the pockets of a long coat. "He was sort of hunched up, as though walking in the rain. I looked again and he was gone. I had just seen a ghost. When I went in to tell Sally what had happened, I was as white as a sheet! Another time I saw a shadow moving behind me and turned to see the ghostly figure of a woman with curly hair standing there."

Young Daniel was playing with Lego one day when he sensed he was being watched. "I turned round to see the outline of two figures with what looked like a thick white line of energy around them. They were standing in the doorway watching me," he said. The following week he was in the kitchen eating porridge, when he saw the outline of a little terrier with a stubby tail walk through the kitchen and disappear behind the fridge. Again there was a wide white line around him. Daniel would sometimes glimpse a man's legs walking up the stairs, but there was never any sound. "It was like I had gone deaf," he said.

A transparent bubble

Son, Ben, saw the ghost of an elderly man with a hunched back, who was standing with his hand on the banister. Some mornings at 7am, what he described as a 'transparent bubble' would appear in his room. "I was so fascinated that I would sit by my bedroom door and watch for it," he said.

One night, Sally and Steven heard a loud knock on their bedroom door just after 10pm and someone walked in. Thinking one of the children was out of bed, Steven went to check, but they were fast asleep. Another night when he was getting undressed, Steven felt a heavy shove in the chest and something pushed him over. "I could feel a pair of hands, and I think they were a woman's hands, in the middle of my chest; it felt like I had been hit by a train. I was shaking like a leaf when I went to tell Sally what had just happened. I felt that whatever was there was singling me out. These attacks became more frequent and I started to hate the atmosphere in the house. I dreaded coming home," admitted Steven. "I could feel cold spots in the lounge, and sometimes

Upper Ryde in 1808. The old Chapel of St Thomas can been seen on the left.

in the bathroom the cold was so intense that I could see my breath. I did not want to be alone in that house. I felt unwelcome and unwanted there."

One morning Sally went downstairs to find every cupboard and drawer in the kitchen wide open, however she wasn't as perturbed by the strange goings-on as her husband was; quite the reverse. "I loved it there. I found the atmosphere warm and friendly, as though there was someone or something always there with me. I felt quite at ease with the presence and would even chat to it."

A friend who was a police dog handler visited with his German Shepherd, Buster, one evening. "That dog was quite fearless," said Sally. "But when he came in he hated the place, barking and growling non-stop until he was taken out again."

After a year, the builders returned to the houses to check for faults, so the family asked them to look at the bedroom floor where those footstep noises were heard. However, they were unable to make it creak at all. But later that same night those overhead footsteps were back and were louder than ever.

Finally, in desperation, the family turned to the Church for help. After hearing their story, a local priest from nearby St Michael's Church agreed to come round and see what he could do. Sally explained, "Father Mike went into every room, checking everything and blessing the rooms. Then we said a prayer with him, he had a cup of tea and when he left, he told us to keep a Bible open at the Lord's Prayer in the boys' bedroom. As soon as the priest left the place felt different. It sounds strange, but the atmosphere changed and brightened. The oppressive feeling Steve was experiencing vanished, and after that we were hardly troubled by spirits there," said Sally.

"I was not attacked any more, and although we still saw the occasional shadowy figure and heard phantom footsteps, we could live with that," added Steven.

By the time they finally moved out in 1998, the family knew of several other homes nearby where ghosts had also been seen. Neighbours whose house was diagonally next to theirs often saw a figure walking across their kitchen, while other next-door neighbours' children talked of seeing ghosts at the bottom of their stairs. "A number of other people told us that their homes were haunted," said Steven. "As older houses were demolished to make way for our homes, I believe the spirits must have originated there," he added.

Chapter Six

HAUNTED MANORS AND MANSIONS

A GHOST SEEKS FORGIVENESS

The picturesque 'Kynges Towne of Brading' is reputed to be the oldest village on the Island. Nearby, Morton (Anglo-Saxon for 'by the water') was a hamlet on the edge of Brading Harbour, now reclaimed land. Morton, or Brading Manor as it was also known, was originally built in 1249 for the Norman knight, Thomas de Aula. A Tudor longhouse was added later, and the manor substantially rebuilt in 1680.

Refurbished again in the Georgian period, it remains today a charming and graceful home to the Trzebski family, the current owners for almost 50 years, who opened Morton to the public in 1977. Meanwhile, the peaceful gardens are a delightful blend of formality and informality. A vineyard, which has been added to take advantage of the Island's high sunshine hours and light intensity, now produces quality Estate grown and bottled Morton Manor wines.

Naturally, the manor is haunted. How could such a beautiful, historic house not enjoy the company of ghosts? When the Trzebski family bought the old manor, much of it was clad in thick, green ivy, which was damaging the stonework. Janusz Trzebski recalled, "About 30 years ago, when my father decided to strip the ivy off the walls, we uncovered two windows which had been blocked up in the late 1700s, probably when Window Tax was introduced."

As the tax was paid on a house of more than six windows, people would brick up one or two windows over the stated six. In 1792, people with 10-19 windows would pay an annual tax of four shillings (20p)!

Morton Manor at Brading, its wall covered in ivy

"The niches where the old windows once sat had been bricked in, so my father encouraged a wisteria which was growing there to cover the wall in place of the ivy. But indoors, within just a couple of days, strange things began to happen. We would hear footsteps moving about the house between the dining room, hall and library, which all adjoined that wall where the ivy had been removed.

After the ivy was removed these blocked-in windows were revealed

"Doors were slammed, and in a small morning room next to the dining room, my mother, Jane, complained that someone, or something, was watching her. The unseen presence stood so close behind her that she could almost feel it touching her. Then, in the dining room, an oil painting in a heavy gilt frame, which had been securely fastened to the wall, fell onto the floor. This was curious because the string was unbroken, and the picture had apparently jumped over the top of an ornate clock standing on the sideboard below to land, undamaged, on the oak floor.

"After a few days of this my father, John, had had enough. He went outside to the courtyard and said in a loud voice, 'Whoever you are, pack it in! We are doing this work for the benefit of the house,' The ghost must have been listening because it worked. From then on, the disturbances stopped and we have had no trouble since," said Janusz, who tells this tale when visitors ask if the house is haunted. However, the following story has not been shared with visitors. It involves a local psychic who visited Morton in the late 1980s with a friend of Jane Trzebski. Janusz recalled, "She walked around the house and announced that she could feel 'something' in the dining room. Sitting near the fireplace she started noting down what she could feel, using automatic writing. (Automatic writing is an old form of divination in which messages come from the 'Spirit World' through the medium's hand and onto paper)

The psychic produced reams and reams of it, writing at great speed for several minutes. When she had finished she was exhausted and announced that she was in need of a stiff gin!

This oil painting fell to the floor without damaging the ornate clock on the sideboard

"What we read came, apparently, from the unhappy spirit of a previous Lady of the manor who was seeking forgiveness. This Lady, who had been stern, unbending, and a tyrant, had refused to give permission for her maid to wed one of the gardeners at Morton Manor. She now deeply regretted this and was seeking a pardon and closure of the matter.

"We thought this was a bit of a joke, so we certainly never did anything more about it," said Janusz. "The psychic also offered us a copy of what she had written for a mere £25, but we declined. I had all but forgotten the incident until 1992, when I took a party on a tour around the house. When we reached the drawing room, one of the visitors asked if he could speak to me after the tour. He wanted to know where the gardener's cottage was on the estate. I told him we did not have one any more. We used the thatched coach house instead. The man explained that many years ago, his great, great, great-grandfather had worked here as a gardener - until he eloped with one of the maids, after the Lady of the house had refused them permission to marry!

"This story had been passed down through his family, and as this was his first ever visit to the Island, he had been intrigued to see where his ancestors had met and fallen in love." After some research, Janusz believes that the Lady in question may have been Lady Sinclair Denman. She was the wife of Sir Thomas Denman (1779-1854) Lord Chief Justice of the King's Bench and Solicitor General for Queen Caroline when her husband, King George IV, tried unsuccessfully to have their marriage dissolved.

The couple, who rented Morton Manor, may well have been responsible for bricking up those windows. It's possible therefore, that it was Lady Denman's ghost which took such offence when the ivy was removed from that wall. Although a formidable woman in her lifetime, in death she may have come to repent of her actions and by the time the psychic visited, she was ready to seek forgiveness for her harsh behaviour.

A HOUSE TO DIE FOR

Ann O'Connor fell in love with her home at Appuldurcombe, near Wroxall, the first moment she saw it. "It's a house to die for!" she insists. "I have found heaven here."

Originally converted from the remains of an ancient Saxon church, it was substantially rebuilt after an unfortunate accident involving gunpowder and an open fire, some 50 years later in 1567.

Ann, a resident of Guernsey, was visiting the Isle of Wight to research her family history when she discovered Appuldurcombe Lodge, once the Gatehouse to nearby Appuldurcombe House, which is itself a very haunted place. (Read about it in *Ghosts of the Isle of Wight Book Four*)

"It's almost like I was led here," said Ann. "I feel as if I have come home. This is the only place I have ever felt so instantly at ease. I know that the place has changed hands many times over the years so it is possible that former owners have been bothered by the ghosts."

Shortly after she bought the lodge in March 2002, Ann started to hear the sound of children's laughter, and footsteps running about upstairs. "I will often be reading in the sitting room when I hear them upstairs. Piles of photographs and papers I am working on are rifled through and moved. It is like having mischievous children about the place," she said with a smile. "If something vanishes, I just ask 'them' to return it. They always do - eventually," she added.

Her cat, Tabitha, will often stare intently at something unseen and this usually means that 'the boys' as Ann refers to them, are nearby. "The boys don't bother me at all. I am not the least bit spooked by them," she said. She believes that 'the boys' are probably John and George, the two young sons and heirs of Captain of the Island and Constable of Carisbrooke Castle, Richard Worsley, who met a tragic end in the house. The boys, aged eight and nine, were being schooled in the Gatehouse or Porter's Lodge, as it was also known, by the Parson of Godshill. Sadly, one day during an invasion scare, estate servants who were also members of the local militia, were drying gunpowder in the adjoining room. The day was cold and someone, with crass stupidity, had lit a fire. The inevitable happened and a spark ignited the powder barrel. In the resulting explosion, several people, including the young Worsley boys, were killed.

Sir Richard Worsley, in his History of the Isle of Wight, wrote: "These two young gentlemen, being in the lodge at Appledercombe, or

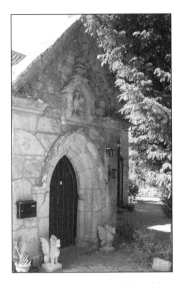

The Saxon origins of the old Gatehouse at Appuldurcombe can clearly be seen here

Gatehouse, where they went to schole, the servants were dryinge of powder there against the general muster, a sparke flewe into the dish, that sett fire to a barrel which stood by, blew up a side of the gatehouse, killed the two children and some others, hurt one James Worsley, a youth, their kinsman and mine, that went to schole with them, who hath often told me this story."

A visit in June 2003 by local psychic Margo Williams helped Ann to discover more about the riddle of who else haunts her house, along with 'the boys'. "She sat herself down and when she had made contact with a spirit here, she started automatic writing. For some 15 minutes she wrote incredibly fast in a very old script, and what she read back was apparently a communication from a lady. This lady, who did not tell us her name, had fallen in love with a James Worsley – possibly the one who was injured in the explosion. After her death she had been happy to linger here through the centuries and did not want to leave.

"I told Margo that if the ghost wished to remain here, I would love to have her around. At this she started writing again. Her words read, 'Thanks be to the lady. I will stay'."

Two young boys were killed in an explosion at the Gatehouse in 1567. Their spirits are heard here.

MORE TALES FROM KNIGHTON GORGES

From the high downs the road drops to a valley. Driving, you come without warning upon two decaying stone pillars, all that remains of a magnificent gateway. Sheep graze as rabbits scuttle among a wilderness of brambles and cow-parsley. You can see, there among the trees, the ivy-shrouded remnant of a broken wall. That is all. But walk carefully. You are walking on haunted ground and the mystery of Knighton Gorges casts an enduring spell.

But has the ancient manor of Knighton Gorges gone forever? Or does it still exist beyond the bounds of space and time? A foolish question, one thinks, standing on a grassy mound where the past is covered by pine trees. And yet...

Knighton Gorges is now recognised as the Island's most haunted place. It exerts a strange fascination for many; including scores of ghost-hunters who gather here every New Year's Eve, in the hope of seeing the old house reappear. The manor was demolished almost two centuries ago, but something definitely lives on there, where a ruined gateway leads to a haunted hill.

As the old house was pulled down many years before it could be captured on film, we must rely on a few contemporary engravings or brief, written descriptions for an impression of what was once said to be "by far the most considerable and beautiful of the ancient mansions of the Island".

Shortly after Knighton Gorges was demolished, in his Historical Guide to the Isle of Wight, published in 1823, John Bullar, wrote: "On the left in a deep vale, stood Knighton House, lately the seat of George Maurice Bisset Esq, but now almost entirely demolished. The following description will show what this house once was:

Open to the south and with a most copious and clear spring rising close under it, stands Knighton House, a very large old building of beautiful grey stone and of very irregular form. One end is totally covered with ivy, which closely invests the wall, roof and chimney. The north front, to which you enter from a small lawn, is all ancient and much broken with projections, with large windows of very good shape. On the south the ground falls so quick, that the garden is in a succession of terraces; and in one part the ground is supported by a high stone wall, built sloping and winding with irregular angles round the hill on which the house stands.

Just at the foot of a steep bank, the spring forms a transparent pool, overhung with willows and shrubs. The view from the south front is pretty.

The present house, though of very respectable antiquity, is modern when compared with some remains in its walls; for on the east side is part of a large and elegant Gothic window, with its tracery still remaining, though obliterated in part by a long stone-mullioned window, of the age of Elizabeth. To what this once belonged, no history of the Island informs us.

The house within is comfortable, but has no striking features. Under a square turret, lower than the rest of the building, and buttressed on the outside, is a very deep dungeon, thirty feet under the floor. The arms of Isabella de Fortibus, last lady of the Island, are in painted glass in one of the windows, but apparently not near so ancient as her time."

The Haunter Haunted

Ghosts and spirits hold no fear for Steve Martin. For two years he was actually a 'ghost' himself on a regular basis when he helped Paranormal Perambulations to stage the popular evening Ghostwalks around Newport.

As a cast member and no stranger to chilling theatrical effects, he would lurk on many a night, dressed in costume, in dark alleys and doorways waiting to step out and scare those brave souls taking part in the spooky walk.

"I stood in graveyards and many other haunted places in pitch darkness and I was never the least bit afraid. It was just a bit of fun for me and I never saw anything supernatural myself – although sometimes people on the walk claimed they did!" he said with a grin.

So when Steve's friend Claire Lawrence suggested they should visit the Island's most haunted place, the long-vanished manor house of Knighton Gorges one February night in 2004, he readily agreed.

But perhaps he had tempted fate once too often, for this time the spirits had turned the tables. They were ready and waiting for him instead!

It was February 29th and after Steve had finished work for the night at a Newport hotel, he drove towards Newchurch with Claire and another friend, Jenna Slater. Although the old house is reputedly most active on New Year's Eve, they wondered if the ghosts might also materialise on a 'leap day' (which only happens every four years).

Arriving at Knighton Shute around 11.30pm on a clear, frosty and bright moonlit night, Steve parked in front of the massive stone gateposts and got out of the car with Claire. Jenna decided to remain in the car - wisely as it turns out - with the radio on, the doors locked, and headlights on.

"Everything was still and silent," said Steve. "We climbed over the wooden gate (despite a sign saying it was private property), and walked up the track. Suddenly I felt that someone else was there with us. Over to our right, about fifty feet away, a figure was moving across the grass towards us.

"At first I thought it was someone coming to tell us off for trespassing. Then I noticed it was not a person, but a dark grey, shadowy figure, moving silently through a low lake of white mist. I had the impression that it was a man wearing a tall hat with a brim. However, I couldn't make out his features."

Suddenly Claire screamed. She was thoroughly unnerved by now and she shouted at the approaching figure to go away. It didn't react, and seemed unaware of the trespassers, neither looking up nor breaking its stride as it moved across the frosty ground towards them.

"Suddenly the figure faded away and we were alone again. We bolted for the gate and scrambled over it a lot faster this time. I was in such a rush that I shot past the car and had to run back to it!

"We got in and locked the doors then just looked at one another. We couldn't believe what had just happened. But we had both seen it, incredible as it seems. After all those times when I dressed up as a ghost to frighten people, the spirits were getting their own back. I probably deserved it."

A Stovepipe Hat

Could this figure in the tall hat be the same one seen by Sybil Wiggins one winter's night in the late 1980s, as Sybil, who now lives at West Place, Ryde, drove home to Sandford with her late husband, after an evening with friends?

Leaving the Downs road they turned into Knighton Shute, passing the old stone gateposts which once led to Knighton Gorges. Outlined ahead in the car headlights, Sybil could see the figure of a man who was walking along the side of the road in the same direction they were travelling.

"I could see him very clearly. He looked solid and was wearing a long, dark coat with a shoulder cape. On his head was a tall, dark, stovepipe hat with a curly brim. I took my eyes off the road and said to my husband who was driving, 'Look at that man, he must be in fancy dress.'

"But my husband didn't know what I was talking about. He couldn't see the figure at all. As we drew closer, the man started to fade away and by the time we were level he had disappeared completely. I could hardly believe it. The figure had looked so very real to me. Although it happened a long time ago, I have never forgotten it.

"At the time I had no idea that the area was supposed to be haunted. I told several friends what I had seen, most of them just laughed at me. But I know it did happen," insisted Sybil.

Ghost Hunters Get Lucky

A trio of intrepid ghost hunters got more than they bargained for during a midnight visit to Knighton Gorges one winter's night in 2002. And when the group's sceptic came face to face with a ghost he was physically sick with shock.

One of the trio, Donna Froment of West Street, Newport, explained, "A group of us would often go out ghost hunting at night to some of the Island's most haunted places. On this occasion as we returned from Sandown, we decided to drive past Knighton Gorges.

The road was empty and there were no other vehicles about as we stopped the car in the entrance to a field with the headlights illuminating the old gateposts almost opposite. There, in the lights we could see the figure of a man who was standing next to the right hand gatepost.

"We drove forwards for a closer look at him. He was wearing a high, black top-hat, a dark, knee-length cloak or cape, and a dark waistcoat, on which we could see a gold watch chain hanging from a pocket. I think he had a moustache. He appeared solid, as he stood there, silent and still.

"We weren't brave enough to get out of the car, so we turned the car sideways to get closer still to the figure. As the headlights moved off him, we shone a torch to keep him in view.

Then as our front seat passenger wound down his window, shouting 'Hello. Hello' and talking to the figure, it faded away before our eyes."

Suddenly, to their amazement, a misty shape, like dark smoke, started to form into a figure right beside the passenger door of the car in the dark, deserted lane. "We were off like a shot. This was just too weird and scary," said Donna. "We had to stop further up the road to let our passenger out of the car to be sick. He was the one who didn't believe in ghosts, and was so shocked to actually see one that he threw up!"

There are Stone Creatures!

Russell Chantler of Sandown moved to the Island from Kent in April 2003, and that summer he went out for a drive with a friend one sunny afternoon. "On our way back to Sandown, my friend Geoff Holt, an Island resident for many years, directed me to Knighton Gorges. As we drove down the dark Knighton Shute from the Downs, the road was flanked by leafy trees which blocked out the bright sunshine. I could sense it was a very eerie place, as goosebumps appeared on my arms.

"Geoff asked what I saw as we passed a driveway and some old stone gateposts. I looked quickly to my left and told him that I had seen two old stone posts with animal gargoyles on the top.

"Geoff looked shocked and asked if I was positive of what I had seen. He told me to stop the car and we reversed up the road to the entrance to Knighton Gorges. But this time when I looked at the old stone gateposts I couldn't see the stone creatures there.

"Then Geoff told me that other people had seen these creatures on the gateposts, although there's nothing there. When we got back to his house, we had a coffee, and Geoff produced the Original Ghosts of the Isle of Wight book, containing the story of Knighton Gorges and the gateposts. I shuddered while reading the details. I definitely saw them and I will never forget that day in the summer of 2003."

Old Stone Lions

Island-born Freddie Morris knows Knighton Gorges well. At the tender age of 18 months, he moved with his parents in 1956 to an old house near the waterworks, once part of the Knighton estate, when his father took a job at nearby Knighton Farm.

"When I was about two-years-old I was left alone in the front room with my toys, whilst my mother was busy in the scullery. A very tall lady, (or so she seemed) dressed in black, entered the room and touched me on the forehead. I screamed as it hurt, and although I told my mother the lady burnt me, I think now it may have been extreme cold I felt. I still have a vague memory of this incident and remember my mother rushing into the room, thinking I must have had an accident. Discussing

The old stone gate posts which led to the long-vanished manor house of Knighton Gorges. This photograph taken in the 1920s clearly shows no stone creatures.

this with her many years later, she told me that when she ran in she had been actually aware of 'something' black moving in the room.

"My mother sometimes used to walk my younger sister and me past the old entrance to Knighton Gorges. Although I was sometimes in my pushchair, I distinctly remember seeing the stone lions on top of the gateposts. It was a good many years before anyone could convince me that they weren't really there. I know I saw them!"

A Panic Attack

Steve Cook of High Street, Wroxall, and a friend, Fran Price, had read all about the haunted Knighton Gorges site but had never visited there - until one August night in 2003, when they set out at 10pm armed with dowsing rods and a camera.

"I parked across the road from the gateposts with the car pointing back up Knighton Shute," explained Steve. "We also left the car headlights on to give us some ambient light as we went to explore. I held the copper dowsing rods, which started spinning around wildly as I neared the old stone gateposts. It may have just been imagination, but the place definitely felt 'charged' and spooky."

Then Fran held the rods, mentally asking if there were any spirits about. She said, "One of the rods immediately swung to the left, then both rods crossed at the base. I felt a sudden pushing sensation. I said, 'I'm sorry, I'm sorry', and backed away, crouching down low to the ground. It was as if I was taking on someone else's feelings and energy. I can't really explain it any more clearly, then I felt such a wave of sadness it was like a panic attack and I wanted to burst into tears."

Steve by now was very concerned for Fran. He could see she was being affected by 'something' at the site and moved quickly to help her back to the car. Starting the engine he raced away up the hill, and didn't stop until they were on the main Downs road. There they parked while Fran gradually calmed down. "I felt so silly," she said. "I don't know what came over me. There's definitely an energy and sense of presence at Knighton Gorges which affected me more than I could ever have imagined."

Knighton Gorges House in 1815, drawn by Sir H. C. Englefield

Chapter Seven

GHOSTS OF OSBORNE HOUSE

This first ever chapter on Osborne's ghosts has taken a very long time to write - more than 27 years in fact. That's because since 1977, when the original Ghosts of the Isle of Wight was published - I have been trying, in vain, to persuade people to tell me of their experiences at the house. Although many had interesting stories of ghostly encounters there, custodians and other staff were discouraged from talking about them, either to inquisitive visitors or to paranormal researchers such as myself. My thanks therefore go to all those who have now been brave enough to tell me their stories, to English Heritage and the Manager of Osborne House, Alan Lock, for their help and co-operation.

DEAR BEAUTIFUL OSBORNE

For more than half a century, Osborne House was at the very heart of the British Empire. From this Royal holiday home at East Cowes, much of the world was governed. Monarchs, emperors, nobility, prime ministers, politicians, foreign dignitaries and ambassadors regularly crossed the Solent to the Isle of Wight to visit Queen Victoria when she and her family were in residence there.

Now open to the public and administered by English Heritage, this Royal three-storey seaside villa overlooking the Solent was built by Queen Victoria and Prince Albert on a 1,000-acre estate, which they purchased from Lady Isabella Blachford. Queen Victoria married Prince Albert in 1840 and five years later they bought Osborne, then a relatively small Georgian house. The Queen knew and liked the Island, having visited it as a girl with her widowed mother, the Duchess of Kent.

Victoria's letter to Lord Melbourne from Osborne in 1845 bubbles with excitement at 'Our new and really delightful home. The sea was so blue and calm that the Prince said it was like Naples. We can walk about anywhere by ourselves without being followed and mobbed'.

But the modest house was too small for a growing family, so the neighbouring estate of Barton Manor was also acquired. Old Osborne House was demolished and replaced by an Italianate mansion designed by Prince Albert, with the help of master builder and architect Thomas

In 1829, Osborne was the home of the Blachford family

Cubitt. Two tall towers dominated the landscape and every important window gave views over the Solent and the terraced gardens leading down to the sea. The building was financed from the Queen's own personal funds.

She loved her 'dear beautiful Osborne', which became the Royals' favourite seaside retreat. Ideal for family holidays, it had a private beach where Queen Victoria first swam from a bathing machine in July 1847. Its easy accessibility by train and ferry also enabled the Queen to pay frequent visits at other times of the year. Privy Councils were held there, and many Royal guests entertained.

At Osborne the family could be free from the formalities of Court life in London, which explains the personal affection the Queen had for it, despite the early death of Prince Albert in 1861. The house was a refuge for the widowed Queen, who kept rooms and the grounds exactly as Albert had left them. In these cheerless surroundings, while still in deep mourning, the Prince and Princess of Wales were allowed their honeymoon in March 1863.

Osborne became a favourite place for family holidays once more, when increasing numbers of Royal grandchildren spent summers there. Victoria's eldest and favourite grandchild, Wilhelm of Prussia, who later became Kaiser Wilhelm II, first visited as a child of two in 1861; returning frequently to the 'dear old home' for the next forty years.

In her later life, the Queen took great comfort in the company of her youngest daughter, Princess Beatrice, who lived in the Durbar Wing at Osborne. This area, built in 1890-91, houses the unique and spectacular Durbar Room, built under the direction of Rudyard Kipling's father. This state function room is the setting for the stunning collection of Indian gifts given to the Queen for her Golden and Diamond Jubilees and brought the splendour of India to the home of the Empress of India.

On Christmas Eve 1900, Victoria saw her last Christmas tree lit in the Durbar Room, its candles seeming dim to her 81-year-old eyes. The Queen died, in her own bedroom during the evening of 22 January 1901, supported by the Kaiser and surrounded by her children. Her coffin lay in state in the dining room for ten days, as she had wished - the Kaiser being in charge of the arrangements at Osborne.

Britain's longest serving monarch had reigned for 63 years. It was the end of an era and the last time Osborne House would be a Royal home. A year after the death of his mother, King Edward handed it over to the nation.

Queen Victoria's coffin leaving East Cowes in 1901

The main and household wings were converted into a convalescent home for officers and, in 1903, a Royal Naval College was established in the former stable block. This closed in 1921.

Like the house, the formal Italianate-style gardens at Osborne were designed by Cubitt and Prince Albert. Since English Heritage took over Osborne in 1984, the walled garden that produced fruit and flowers for the household has been restored and the terrace gardens, which have stunning views across the Solent, have been opened to visitors. Osborne House is also a popular film location with many television programmes being filmed there, including the blockbuster film 'Mrs Brown' starring Judi Dench and Billy Connolly.

HE WALKED THROUGH THE DOOR!

When Beryl Mackenzie started work as a custodian at Osborne House, it was, she declared, the best job she'd ever had. Beryl worked at the house and convalescent home for 14 years, including four as senior custodian, until she retired in 2000. Beryl now lives at Wootton, within sight of the towers of Osborne House.

"I knew that house like the back of my hand and I loved my time there," she said. "Often as a senior custodian I had to check the entire building, from the flag tower to the basement, once visitors had left, to make sure it was locked and secure for the night. I spent many, many hours in Queen Victoria's bedroom - where she died - but I never felt her presence there, which is perhaps surprising, because she was such a strong personality. In fact the question most frequently asked by visitors was, 'Is the house haunted?' Everyone wanted to hear about ghosts. But we had been instructed to tell them, 'No, there are no ghosts here'!"

A ghost emerged through this bedroom door

That wasn't true, however, as Beryl now confirms. She and several other staff - not to mention some astonished visitors - had supernatural encounters at the house, which defy all rational explanation.

One brief encounter is still etched in her memory. "I was on duty in the Royal nurseries on the top floor. It was a lovely, sunny, late summer's afternoon in the early 1990s, and the house was quiet with very few visitors around. One of our set positions was to stand in the doorway recess so we could see people in the corridors. I was waiting there for visitors to come out of the nursery so that I could direct them back down the stairs.

"On my right was another recessed doorway leading to a locked room which wasn't open to the public. I had never had the key to this room - or even been inside it. The doorways here were deeply recessed, and the walls were very thick.

"I suddenly glimpsed a movement on my right, as someone emerged from the doorway next to me into the corridor. I saw white shirt cuffs, three or four inches long, a pale, silvery-grey suit and narrow trousers. As the figure stepped out, I said, 'Can I help you?' but as I spoke, he stepped back, quickly, and disappeared again, right through the door." Beryl was astonished.

"I can still see it to this day, even after all this time. I could hardly believe my eyes. What I actually saw was his right arm and leg, which emerged as though he was stepping through the doorway. There was no sound at all. I would estimate he was about 5ft 3ins tall and the portion of his body I did see appeared completely solid in the bright sunlight coming in through the glass dome of the roof above. I was not at all frightened – it was completely fascinating. I just wish I hadn't spoken out when I did. Perhaps I would have got to see all of him!"

Beryl later learned that the locked room from which the ghostly figure had emerged, was the bedroom used by Queen Victoria's youngest, delicate haemophiliac son, Prince Leopold. Born in 1853, Leopold Duke of Albany was a semi-invalid all his life. Despite his uncertain health, which kept him, in the Queen's words 'lame and shaky' he married in 1882 and fathered two children before suffering a final - and fatal - haemorrhage two years later.

On another occasion, Beryl was locking up after the visitors had left for the day. "The place was empty and I was up on the top floor working my way down. As I set off downstairs I heard a door open on the nursery floor above. Thinking it must be one of the other custodians I shouted out, 'For goodness sake, what on earth are you doing up there? I'm locking up.' I turned, but there was nobody there. Yet I knew I was being watched. I had such a strong sense of a presence on that top floor."

A FATAL FALL

Richard Underwood was alone in his office on the lower ground floor of the Osborne House convalescent home, which looked out onto a grass courtyard. The year was 1983. He was the only member of staff on duty as it was Saturday and the house was closed to the public. However, as the Head Custodian at Osborne House since 1980, he was used to working odd hours.

Next to his office was a steep, stone staircase leading to the floor above. This was usually roped off because it was considered so dangerous. Suddenly, Richard heard a scream and a horrible thud. Assuming there had been an accident on that staircase, he rushed outside to help whoever had fallen.

"I thought one of the girls from the nursing home must have tumbled down the stairs, and knowing how nasty and steep they were, I was afraid her injuries could be serious," he said. But once outside, there was no sign of anybody - or indeed any body! The courtyard and staircase were empty. "I was very puzzled because there had been no doubt in my mind that someone had fallen. That's why I rushed out."

In Victorian times, this area known as the "cross-passage" had joined the main household dining room to the corridor where Queen Victoria's audience room and receiving chambers were situated. Richard later learned that a parlour maid had been killed in a fall on that very staircase in the 1880s. Was the scream and sickening thud he heard that day, a ghostly echo of that tragedy which has been all but forgotten?

During his 13 years at Osborne, Richard, who now runs an antique shop in Cowes, had one further brush with the supernatural in 1990. When he became Head Custodian of the Royal Apartments, he was given an office in the main house above the Durbar Room, in what had once been the apartment used by Princess Beatrice and her husband, Prince Henry of Battenburg. Richard recalled, "It was about 1pm on a

A ghostly woman stood at this window

sunny summer's day and the rest of the staff had gone to lunch. As I walked along the main corridor, I saw a woman dressed all in black, standing at the window in Princess Beatrice's former bedroom. She was looking out across the lawns. Because we used this as a sitting room for visitors, I thought little of it at the time. The woman was wearing a late Victorian or early Edwardian costume, so I assumed we had a film crew in the house making a period drama. I went into my office to put some papers away, then returned to the sitting room to introduce myself to the lady who was waiting there.

"To my surprise the room was empty. As she hadn't come past my office, I went to the security checkpoint at the foot of the stairs to find out where she had gone, only to be told no-one had been past the guards and no film crews were in the house that day."

A YOUNG INDIAN BOY

One day, custodian Joan Downer called Richard downstairs to meet a woman who claimed she had been followed by a little ghost-boy. The middle-aged visitor, who explained that she was psychic, said the spirit of a young Indian boy, who told her his name was Kabul, had accompanied her as she walked around the house. This apparition apparently spent much time 'on duty' outside the Horn Room, in the corridor which leads to the Durbar Room.

The visitor also asked Richard why the upholstery in the state apartments had been replaced in gold material when it had originally been red silk damask (according to a scene she pictured in her mind). "At that time the room was upholstered in gold fabric," confirmed Richard. "When we researched this we discovered the original furniture and drapery was actually red silk. This has since been rectified."

So who was that young Indian boy? Queen Victoria was fascinated by the Indian culture and had a large Indian-born staff at Osborne. The Waiting Room where this little spirit was 'on duty' is also known as the Horn Room, because it contains furniture made from antlers and animal horns. The Durbar Room is reached through the Durbar Corridor where there are many pictures of Indians including Abdul Karim, a personal secretary to the Queen who also taught her to speak Hindustani.

The Durbar room takes its name from a Hindi word darbar, originally meaning the court of a native ruler or governor in India, or a formal court reception. Built also for state banquets, the elaborate decoration with its carvings in the Indian-style is a reminder that Victoria was Empress of India, a title she held from 1876.

It was here in the Durbar room, that Senior Custodian David Rowan had one of several strange experiences with a 'touchy' ghost during his 16 years at Osborne House. David who opened a sweet and tobacconist shop in Cowes after leaving Osborne, said, "When I first started working there, I was put on duty in the Durbar Room. It was late in the afternoon, towards the end of the season in October. Most of the visitors had left and as I was alone in the room, I took the opportunity to examine the display cabinets that house some of the many gifts the Queen received on the occasions of her Golden and Diamond Jubilees.

"Suddenly I felt a hand on my right shoulder. I instantly said, 'Stop messing around!' thinking one of the lads from security had crept up on me. But as I swung round, I realised I was alone. The Durbar Room was empty. It was a light touch, a gentle pressure, but it definitely felt like a hand on me," said David.

A couple of years later he felt that hand on his shoulder again - this time in the Grand Corridor, which is on the ground floor of Osborne House. Once again it was October, the end of the season, and late in the afternoon. "It was a slack period, no one was around and it was quite chilly (in fact it was always cold in that corridor). I was looking at the huge statue of Winged Victory there when I suddenly felt a hand on my left shoulder. I thought it was one of the other custodians or a member of security. But when I turned around, yet again there was no one there.

"A year later I was on my rounds locking up, when I had another strange experience," recalled David. "Once the house was closed for the night, it was my job as senior custodian to check that every door was locked and all the shutters were secure. This was before the Royal nurseries on the top floor were opened to the public and they were always kept locked.

"I had checked the doors on every floor, one by one, including the private apartments and offices above the Durbar Room, when I heard a door open and close in the nursery wing. I thought, 'Who the hell is that? There's no-one else here.' But when I checked again, the doors were locked and secure. I was definitely quite alone in the house."

You look like you've seen a ghost!

David's most unusual encounter with one of Osborne's ghosts happened when he was with fellow senior custodian Beryl Mackenzie, after the last visitors had left for the day. "We had been looking after the private apartments together and at about 4.30pm she said, 'Let's have a sit down in the alcove for a few minutes.'

"On the way there I checked that the Queen's sitting room and Prince Albert's dressing room were both empty and the window shutters were drawn. As I looked through the doorway, my tie was suddenly yanked straight out in front of me. Instinctively, I grabbed it back - and I had to tug quite hard before whatever was pulling it let go. It was incredible. When I reached Beryl I was white and shaking. 'What's the matter?' she asked, 'You look like you've seen a ghost'!"

Visitors are always interested in the subject of ghosts at Osborne. Sometimes they tell staff of strange figures in old-fashioned clothes which they have seen. Usually this is because actors are filming costume dramas in the house and grounds. However not every reported sighting is so easily explained.

In the late 1980s a custodian was on duty in the first floor Royal apartments, when a visitor who was coming out of the Queen's bedroom turned to him and inquired, "Can we go upstairs now?" (This was in the days when the top floor was out of bounds).

When the custodian explained there was no public access to the top floor, the visitor was surprised. "Well there is someone up there. I can see a child in a sailor suit playing upstairs," she said.

Security guards are not easily spooked, but long hours spent on duty in the empty house at night have produced a few stories of ghosts and the

Is the Horn Room haunted?

supernatural. One man insisted there was a 'funny feeling' near the Table Deckers' Room, used by staff who decorated tables for grand functions and banquets. This sensation may have had its origins in the suicide of a maid who hung herself there in Victorian times. Another guard hated going past the Horn Room, insisting there was a strong presence there. A few visitors too, have glimpsed 'something untoward' which darts quickly out of sight, in that little room. Perhaps this isn't just imagination, for this was the room favoured by Queen Victoria and her Highland servant John Brown during numerous Spiritualist séances, when they attempted to make contact with the Queen's late husband, Prince Albert. Today, the Horn Room is kept closed to protect its original nineteenth-century carpet, wallpaper, and the remarkable collection of antler furniture, bought by the Prince in 1846.

Despite his brushes with the supernatural at Osborne, David remembers it as a wonderful place to work. "Once the visitors and staff had gone and you were on your own, the house seemed, in some indefinable way, to relax. It had a distinct character of its own and there was quite a magical feeling there. I like to think that whatever ghosts still haunt the house are happy to remain there," he said with a smile.

A STRONG FRAGRANCE

Other custodians have their own stories to tell about Osborne's ghosts. One often noticed the distinctive sweet smell of jasmine, which would waft about at the foot of the main staircase. It was a phenomenon she often commented on to fellow staff members. Then, one day she learned that jasmine had been Queen Victoria's favourite perfume.

Another strong fragrance, which is noticed by staff and visitors alike, is orange blossom, a very sweet perfume that sometimes fills the Queen's bedroom with its agreeable scent. Daphne Shambrook of Osborne Road, East Cowes, who worked at Osborne House for 15 years, first as a cleaner and later as a custodian, smelled the distinctive odour in that room on many occasions.

"I would notice it first thing in the morning when I was opening the rooms up, and sometimes it would linger all day. Visitors would comment, 'What a lovely smell there is in here.' I would just smile and agree. It was as if there was a strong room freshener there. The smell would hit you as you opened the room from the Queen's dressing room. Occasionally, there was a real sense of Victoria's presence in there too. Some mornings I would walk in and say, 'She's here today'."

This was echoed by Jenny Ebbs who smelled that fragrant orange blossom four times during the 13 years she worked as a custodian at Osborne, before retiring in 2003. "It was glorious," said Jenny. "It only happened to me on those few occasions in the Queen's bedroom. I never saw her spirit but could feel her presence was linked in some way to the perfume. Once there was a visitor with me when it happened, and she commented on the lovely smell. There was such a happy feeling that I couldn't stop smiling when perfume filled the room."

When Daphne worked as a cleaning supervisor, she was let into the house by security staff at 6.30am. It was her job to open the internal doors which custodians had locked the previous night. One morning, when she was alone on the first floor above the Durbar corridor, she felt a hand on her shoulder. "I thought it was one of the security guards messing about," said Daphne. "It was a very firm touch; definitely a hand I could feel. But when I looked round, no-one was there."

Daphne is also aware that custodians and visitors have reported seeing a ghostly figure on the top landing, near the Royal nurseries. "A lot of people have glimpsed a man's figure walking along that corridor. We think it is Prince Leopold, although we have not been able to make out his features. It's known that the Prince spent a lot of time up there, and this figure has been seen disappearing through the closed door of Leopold's room.

"I know this was still happening as recently as 2003, when people saw a fleeting dark shadow moving along the landing and through a locked door. There have also been more recent sightings of another of Osborne's ghosts – that little Indian boy, aged 10 or 11 years, who is seen

coming down a flight of stairs and along the Durbar Corridor.
"Visitors would say, 'How nice that you have put someone in costume!' Of course we had done no such thing. However, all the reports would tally. They described a solid-seeming young boy, wearing a turban, a long, greenish-blue jacket and silky trousers."

When custodian Beryl Mackenzie heard of this, it rang a faint bell in her memory. "I believe that in the Queen's later years, when she often used her wheelchair, a young boy was stationed on 'lift duty'. He sat in a recess along the Durbar Corridor, where he could summon two strong footmen to operate her private lift. This lift, one of the very first in Britain to be installed by the Otis Company, ran on pulleys and ropes, rather like a dumb waiter. There was always a child on duty in that corridor, and it was often a little Indian boy," Beryl said.

Although Daphne left Osborne at the end of the 2003 season, she retains a strong affection for the house and goes back there whenever she can. "I used to come to the Island for my holidays and it was always my dream to work at Osborne House. Then the dream came true! This place gets under your skin, it really does. I loved working there. It's very, very odd; there is something about the house that gets to people. It has a warm, welcoming feeling and whatever ghosts linger there are benign and gentle. Osborne was a wonderfully happy family home and the love that Victoria and Albert had for one another, and for their children is there in the very fabric of the place. They adored each other and you can still feel it."

AN UNSEEN PRESENCE

In the early 1990's, Richard McMaster worked for local cleaning company N-VIRO at Osborne House. "Our working hours were from 7.00am till 9.00am and apart from security, we were the only people in the house at that time. Most staff were discouraged from talking of ghosts and the official line was that Osborne was not haunted. However, just once, I had a strange experience at the foot of the main staircase.

"I worked at Osborne for two seasons and my duties involved cleaning the security room, the Durbar Room and the Durbar Corridor, all the way through to the main staircase. This staircase was the last area I cleaned - as all the other cleaners were using it - so this seemed to make sense. Now I'm not a person to believe in ghosts but this was weird. I finished cleaning the main corridor then moved my backpack vacuum cleaner extension lead from the corridor to the billiard room. As I plugged in I was aware of an unseen presence. I don't mean just a ghost; it was something more frightening. I was standing at the foot of the staircase facing upstairs when I sensed a presence behind me. I was certain there was someone or something watching me; I could physically feel I was being observed. I turned quickly but whatever it was had disappeared. I broke out into a sweat and went to find some company.

"Many of the other staff greeted my story with scorn. However, I never felt quite alone again when I was cleaning at Osborne, and I was always on my guard when doing that same job again. I don't scare easily. I'm 6ft 4ins tall and have never been that frightened in my life. I guess you could say that when I turned around I expected to see someone, a fellow cleaner or security guard who had crept up to give me a fright. The last thing I expected to see was nothing at all. I don't believe in ghosts, but this was something quite uncanny. It was the only time I ever experienced anything. Osborne House was a fantastic place to work, I felt so privileged to be there, when the place was otherwise empty."

AN OLD-FASHIONED BUTLER

Richard Clark of Freshwater who worked as custodian from 1991 until October 2003 is equally passionate about Osborne's charms, and has amassed a large collection of Osborne House memorabilia, postcards and photographs going back many years.

"It is a very special place and I loved it there. The house will always have a soft spot in my heart," he said. However, Richard also admitted, "I always took a cynical view of ghosts; I didn't believe in them at all – until the day I met one at Osborne." For Richard, this 'Road to Damascus' conversion came at about 9.15am, one early autumn morning in late September 2002.

"The previous evening I had left my uniform jacket in the staff room above the Durbar Room, so I went to fetch it. I walked up the back staircase in the Durbar Wing and through the door at the top, closing it behind me. As I re-entered the short side corridor from the staff room, a figure moved past me and walked through the closed door at the top of the stairs that I had just come through. I quickly opened the door, but there was no one there. The figure had passed right in front of me, about seven or eight feet away – and instantly I knew it was a ghost.

"It was the figure of a short man who wasn't solid, but resembled a dark shadow. I wasn't at all frightened, although I was a bit shocked.

Osborne House viewed from the air

Later, when I told my colleagues what I had seen it made my skin crawl. It made such an impression that I can still see it clearly to this day. From his deportment I feel he was someone like an old-fashioned butler, perhaps a member of Princess Beatrice's household, for this area of the house was formerly used as her apartments."

Richard also recalled a small but strange event in the Durbar Room, when he was on duty there in late September 2003. "It was late in the day and the room was empty. I was standing just below the Minstrels' Gallery when I felt someone tugging at my trouser leg as if trying to attract my attention. I looked down quickly but there was nothing there."

Between 1974 and 1986 Surgeon Captain Peter Macdonald and his wife Kay lived at Osborne House in an apartment on the top floor where the Royal nurseries are now open to the public. Although she reports no ghostly encounters during that time, Mrs Macdonald describes her time there as a wonderful privilege.

"We occupied the top floor nurseries and the whole time we were there I was conscious of a happy and welcoming atmosphere. Osborne was clearly an extremely happy family home for Albert, Victoria, and their children and they were very good, caring parents. If I had ever seen a ghost there I would like it to have been the little vision of a giggling red-haired Princess Beatrice, the youngest of the Royal princesses, darting round a corner in front of me," said Kay wistfully.

THE GRIMACING GIRL

For Sally Cooper of Elm Grove, Newport, whose job it is to care for the Royal Collection of memorabilia and treasures, working at Osborne House is a joy and privilege. As an Historic Contents Carer since 1997, she is often called upon to work alone and when the house is closed, inspecting and cleaning some of Osborne's 20,000 priceless artefacts and checking the sophisticated environmental system which monitors light, temperature and humidity levels.

While cleaning a fireplace in the Royal day nursery late one afternoon, Sally looked up in surprise to see a young girl peering from the night nursery around the side of the mantelpiece at her. The pale-faced girl in her early teens, had black plaited hair, red lips, and wore a gingham-patterned or striped dress. "She was only visible for a brief second, but I saw her very clearly before she vanished. She looked right at me and grimaced. It was not very pleasant," said Sally.

While working alone on that top floor when the house is closed, she sometimes hears the sound of voices muttering and mumbling in the empty house. The words are too low and indistinct to make out, but they're audible all the same, Sally insists. And early in the morning when at the museum at Swiss Cottage, she often sees someone - or something - moving out of the corner of her eye, and a dark shape that flits past the doorway. But such phenomena don't worry Sally, who's been psychic since she was a child.

"Osborne is a wonderful place to work. Early in the morning and late in the afternoon, particularly when all the visitors have left, the atmosphere changes. The house comes alive. It is almost like an entity. At Christmas it really loves being decorated with pine trees, garlands and cards, you can actually feel it become a warm, happy family home once more."

A GIFT TO THE NATION

After Queen Victoria's death in 1901, her eldest son, King Edward VII lost little time in ridding himself of the estate - by presenting it to the nation. Although the Queen left Osborne to all her children, Edward had no liking for the place. The King explained that because Osborne was sacred to the memory of his late mother, he would be unable to make adequate use of it as a Royal residence. With the exception of the apartments Her Majesty had occupied, which would be opened to the public, he requested the rest of the estate should be converted into 'a Convalescent Home for Officers of the Navy and Army, whose health has been impaired in rendering service to their country'. Thus, the King Edward VII Convalescent Home for Officers was opened by the King on 4 July 1903.

Officers at their remedial exercises

The admission terms were broadened in 1923 to include male civil servants, while in 1948 women officers in the forces were admitted for the first time. By 1950, up to 50 officers could be accommodated at Osborne although psychiatric, incurable patients or those with active tuberculosis weren't admitted. Medical attention was largely free, and numerous therapies including physiotherapy, massage and a hot pool were also available. Resident officers were invited to become honorary members of several sailing clubs and could use the private nine-hole golf course and bathing beach at Osborne. There was a programme of entertainment with concerts, films and dances. Rough shooting was available on the estate, but it was stipulated that 'officers should bring their own guns'.

Over almost a century, thousands of people became lifelong residents or short-term convalescents at the King Edward VII Home. But, by the dawn of the new Millennium, its days were numbered. The home closed for good on 31 October 2000 (Halloween). But what of its ghosts?

Over the years many staff - and some residents - were aware the home was haunted. Some parts of the old building were best avoided after dark; and night staff would make long detours rather than use a certain top floor corridor known as the 'cross-passage'.

FIGURE IN A WHITE BALL GOWN

Heather Pett of Church Road, Wootton, worked as a nursing auxiliary at the convalescent home for eight years, until it was closed. She met a ghost there at 7pm one winter's evening, when she was alone in that top corridor.

Heather recalls, "The residents had gone downstairs for dinner and I was preparing their rooms for the night. As I walked down the corridor, I felt the hairs on the back of my neck rising and I shivered. I had a strong sensation that there was something behind me; I turned and saw what looked like a white dress floating down the corridor, about two or three yards behind me. I couldn't see a head or arms on the figure, just a long, white ball gown swaying soundlessly as it moved towards me.

"I shot down the corridor to the lift as fast as my legs would carry me. I wish now that I had looked more closely at the apparition. But at the time I couldn't get away fast enough. When I got out of the lift on the next floor I must have been deathly white, because when I bumped into Suzanne, another member of staff, she asked, 'What on earth's happened? You're as white as a sheet .' When I told her I had just seen a ghost she said, 'I thought so!'" recalled Heather.

A resident in the home whose room was on that top 'cross-passage' corridor, sometimes told staff he had seen a 'white lady' in there. So a couple of days later Heather spoke to him to compare notes on whether the apparition was the same one she had seen. Yes it was, the patient confirmed.

A FEELING OF DREAD

Sandra Norris knows Osborne House well, because for much of her childhood she lived in New Barn Lodge, where her mother provided bed and breakfast for the families of officers staying at Osborne. Sandra also spent 12 years as a nursing auxiliary at the convalescent home, working night shifts for much of that time. Her introduction to its ghostly residents came soon after she started working there.

Sandra recalled, "Shortly after midnight when we had settled all the residents for the night, the Sister in charge said I should have a rest myself. She told me to use one of the empty rooms off the 'cross-passage', so I made myself comfortable in a chair. I had only been there a few minutes when a horrible sensation of dread and unaccountable fear came over me. I switched on the light, but the feeling persisted.

"I knew I had to get out immediately, but I couldn't bring myself to run across the room to the door. Instead I flattened myself against the wall and crept out that way. When I rushed to the staff room, they were waiting for me, laughing. All the night staff knew about that room - that there was something very unpleasant in there - and I had been deliberately sent in to see how long I would last!

"The other staff told me that room was well-known. It was always so very cold and had a heavy, oppressive feeling of dread. It was not only avoided by staff. Residents and patients too, made excuses to be moved whenever they were allocated that room. Nobody wanted to stay there."

A few years before the home was closed, major renovation works were undertaken to enlarge rooms and provide en-suite facilities for residents. That room became the Duty room and all the fittings and furniture, including a huge old wardrobe, were moved into the room opposite. This was where Sandra was sent for her break one night.

She recalled, "I made myself comfortable and was dozing, when suddenly there was a massive banging noise. I almost jumped out of my skin. I left the light on and lay down again. The sounds started once more and I thought it must be the Victorian plumbing system knocking, but every time I moved towards them, the noises stopped abruptly. I went back to the Duty room and told Sister. She was from the 'old school' and briskly warned me not to be so silly."

To show Sandra there was nothing wrong with the room, Sister returned with her and told her to turn off the light. A few moments later the banging started again, this time in the adjoining, locked and empty room, whose door was hidden by that huge old wardrobe. As the intrepid Sister walked towards it the hammering began again, louder than ever. Both women fled.

Was that old wardrobe and the other furniture from the original haunted room responsible for the disturbances? Sandra doesn't know. Significantly, once the haunted room was cleared of furniture and re-decorated, the coldness and feeling of dread lifted.

During her time at Osborne, Sandra was aware of other haunted areas, including a corridor in the Spur Wing which was always cold, even on the hottest of days. Once part of the Duchess of Kent's (Queen Victoria's mother) apartments, some staff refused to go in there alone. They were always watched by an unseen, but strong presence there, they complained.

A security guard was crossing the deserted top landing one night, when he heard a woman's voice softly calling 'Isabella, Isabella'. No-one with that name was working or resident in the home at the time – but one did once live at Osborne – she was Lady Isabella Blachford, who sold Osborne House to Queen Victoria.

One consciencious doctor even continued on his rounds, long after he was dead. Sister was opening doors and checking on the patients one night and although it was very late, one convalescent was still wide awake. "Hello Sister, do come in," he told her. "And bring that gentleman with you." Nonplussed, she asked who he meant. "Why, that doctor in the white coat standing right behind you!" replied the patient.

DOWN IN THE BASEMENTS

Down in the the extensive basements where the kitchens, storerooms, Chapel and Physiotherapy Department were located, strange happenings are not uncommon, particularly at night. When the house was quiet, staff would hear footsteps on the flagstones and the chatter of ghostly voices – an echo through time from long-dead maids and servants who once belonged to the Royal Household.

A security guard told of his shock one night when he heard the 'tap tap' of footsteps approaching him across the stone floor. As he stood there, the invisible presence walked right past him; the sound of those footsteps receded into the distance and all was silent once more.

After dropping her husband off to catch a ferry, Sheila West went in to work early at 5.15am one winter morning in 1998. Usually she started at 6am, so the basement area was empty at that time in the morning and

Queen Victoria's favourite home. The Royal Apartments are on the right of the picture.

she had the domestic staff room in the lower 'cross-passage' to herself.

"The place was silent. Suddenly, I heard footsteps on the stone floor outside. At first I thought it was the security guards changing shift, then I realised they weren't due until 6am. The sound I could hear was the 'tippy-toe' noise of a woman's small footsteps ringing out clearly in the silence of the empty basement."

Daphne Shambrook also heard those footsteps one morning after she and her cleaning team had finished their shift. "We were just being nosy really. One of the security men took us on a tour of the basement when there was no one else around. We all heard a woman's footsteps walking along the flagstone floor, although we couldn't see anybody there. When we asked what on earth it was, the security man just laughed and told us, 'Oh it's just the ghosts. We hear them all the time; we are used to it by now!'

"We had hardly recovered from that, when we saw an old, recessed cupboard open and shut on its own. Nobody was near it when the wooden door swung open, then closed again. It was just another of those odd things that happen in that basement at Osborne," laughed Daphne.

ECHOES OF CHILDHOOD PLAY

Half-a-mile to the east of the main house is the little wooden Swiss Cottage. Constructed in 1853-4, it was based on a traditional Austrian Tyrolean design as a playhouse for the Royal children who were expected to play purposefully there, tending their gardens and entertaining their parents to tea. The area was actually given to the children in 1850 as a place where they could grow fruit, flowers and vegetables, and sell them at commercial rates to their father, the Prince Consort.

Under the Prince's tuition the young princes and princesses learned the rudiments of housekeeping and cookery there, also displaying their growing natural history, geology and souvenir collections. The Victoria Fort and Albert Barracks, a miniature fort complete with earthworks, stands behind the cottage. This was a great favourite with the young princes, especially Prince Arthur, who was later to become Field Marshal the Duke of Connaught.

For 27 years until 1994, Brian Gregory lived at Swiss Cottage as gardener and caretaker, while his wife looked after the cottage and museum. "We were there all year round, even when the main house and grounds were closed to visitors for the winter. We had five cats and at least a hundred pipistrelle bats, which lived in the loft – but we never saw or heard any ghosts. It was a lovely, warm, happy place to live and work. It was such a privilege to be there. It certainly wasn't lonely, for many an evening the officers and patients from the convalescent home would drop in for a chat. I did hear other people mention ghosts but they never showed themselves to me," said Brian.

But in part of those grounds where the young princes and princesses spent many happy hours, faint echoes of their laughter are still heard by some staff. Gardener Adrian Wright has heard those haunting faint ripples from the past reverberating through time. Island-born Adrian, who lives at Cowes, has worked for English Heritage since 1986 as groundsman and gardener at several properties, including Carisbrooke Castle and Appuldurcombe House. Now based all-year-round at Osborne House, he tends the gardens at Swiss Cottage, watching the seasons change in their timeless way. "Osborne House is an incredible place to work. I feel so privileged to be there. It really gets under your skin. It's like becoming a part of the history of the Osborne Estate working here, like generations before have done."

A few years ago in springtime, two custodians stationed in The Meadow heard laughter and voices of unseen children playing by the Barracks. Not an unusual occurrence at the little fort, but this was early in the day, before the house was open or any visitors had arrived. Both custodians hurried towards the unexpected sound, moving in opposite directions around the fort. When they met up again at the Barracks they were very surprised that they hadn't seen the children anywhere.

On another occasion Adrian was on his morning break in the gardeners' hut when he and a fellow gardener heard the distinctive sound of footsteps on the gravel path behind. This time it was winter and the house was closed to the public. Thinking it must be one of the security staff approaching, both men went out to see who was there. The garden was empty.

One beautiful day in spring 2002, Adrian was enjoying a quiet morning coffee in the gardeners' shed with four fellow staff members. "It was just after 10am on this glorious morning; there was not a hint of a breeze and no visitors had yet arrived. Suddenly, we all heard the sound of children laughing nearby. We were surprised, because none of us had heard the nearby gate to the gardens open or the sound of anyone approaching. I went straight out to see where they were and to open the

Osborne House casts an enduring spell on those who live and work there

main gate for the mini-bus, which brings visitors to Swiss Cottage. However, the gardens were empty, there were no children anywhere. The pedestrian gate was still locked.

"It was happy laughter and we heard it for perhaps ten seconds. I believe it was a recording from the past, an echo of happy times, possibly on a similar glorious spring morning long ago. This was after all, the children's own garden, where they spent much time working on their little plots in their own time and world."

So much for Osborne and its ghosts. The former Royal home casts an enduring spell on those who live and work there, where past and present meet in this most haunting of houses.

The Albion Hotel in Freshwater Bay, pictured in 1990

Chapter Eight

WRAITHS OF THE VILLAGES

TOTLAND GHOST CHILDREN

The sound of excited children running along the beach was nothing out of the ordinary for Ann and Brian. What was unusual however, was when it started happening after dark – and at midnight.

"It was late one night in April 2003, there was a Spring tide and the sea was right out. As we lay in bed talking, I could hear the sound of kids playing outside. Looking at the bedside clock I could see it was almost midnight. Suddenly we both heard the sound of youngsters running across the shingle, and when I drew back the curtains and looked out of the window I could see two kids on the beach," said Ann.

The large beachfront house in which Ann and Brian have a flat was once used as an annexe and staff quarters to the Totland Chalet Hotel on the nearby cliff top, which was demolished in the 1970s.

In the light cast by seafront street lamps outside their home at Totland Bay, Ann could see a boy and girl aged eight or nine, wearing rather old-fashioned clothes, with what she describes as "below the knee bloomers". Both children appeared greyish in colour. They were running around laughing and shouting, and Ann, who was suddenly struck by the strangeness of the scene, wondered where their parents were.

"I turned to Brian and said 'Where on earth are their parents?' As I looked again they had gone. The beach was empty and silent again."

A few weeks later the couple were out for a late walk along the seafront when they both noticed the same children playing on the beach again. The time was 11.30pm and again the tide was low.

"Out of the corner of his eye, Brian saw what looked like two little shadows by one of the beach huts. They appeared to run through the railings, down the beach and into the sea. I had a better view and could see them full on. They looked like two darkish clouds going into the sea. Although I couldn't see their faces I was looking at a boy and girl. Her hair was in brown ringlets, and both were wearing strange clothes like pyjama bottoms or knickerbockers.

"The road is well lit there and in the street lights we saw them both running along the beach laughing and shouting, as excited children do.

Totland beach in the early 1900s   *Totland beach pictured in the 1950s*

Curiously though, this time we could not hear the shingle crunching as they ran across it. One moment they were there, the next they had vanished and all was quiet again.

"I don't know what we saw or heard but I suspect the children were ghosts," said Ann. "They haven't been back since, but late at night, especially on a still evening when the tide is out, I often find myself listening for them...."

SOUND OF SOBBING

It was a beautiful August night in 1990 and Vincent Santini was still wide awake. He and his wife were spending their honeymoon on the Isle of Wight, at the Albion Hotel in Freshwater Bay. Their room, one of the best in the hotel, had fine views across the bay.

Although his new wife was fast asleep, Vincent lay beside her listening to the sound of the waves on the beach beneath their balcony. The moon was shining and everything was peaceful and still. Then something very odd happened. The sound of the sea stopped and Vincent heard a woman's voice sobbing and crying out a name, although he was unable to make out what the name was. As she paced up and down the beach, Vincent could hear her footsteps crunching on the shingle below.

"I looked down but the beach was empty, although I could still hear her there, calling and crying. She sounded quite distraught and I was really concerned. Suddenly everything stopped and the murmuring sound of the waves began again."

Next morning Vincent mentioned the strange episode to the hotel receptionist. "Ah yes," she said. "Other people sometimes hear her too."

Many years ago, she told Vincent, a young woman threw herself and her baby into the sea at Freshwater Bay. Sadly both were drowned. But at certain times of year her ghost is heard - but never seen - running sobbing along the beach, calling desperately for her dead child.

GHOST IN THE MIRROR

As a senior officer responsible for European and Regional issues at the Island's council, Lesley Williams is a very rational person. So when she woke in the early hours one morning with the feeling that someone unseen was sitting on the end of her bed, she didn't scream or run from the room. She just went back to sleep.

Since then Lesley has been woken several times by the sensation of someone sitting down on her bed. Actually, after moving into her cottage in Crocker Lane, near Niton, in January 1999, Lesley has had a number of unusual experiences there.

"When I first moved in, I couldn't keep mirrors on the walls. All around the cottage they would fall off onto the floor. Sometimes the strings would break; but usually there was no reason for the mirror to have fallen.

"It generally happened in the middle of the night, and when travelling abroad, I notice that whoever haunts my cottage seems to misbehave before I go away - as if in protest."

On one occasion, prior to leaving on another trip, Lesley was lying in the bath when the bathroom mirror, which measures about 18ins by 2ft 6ins, somersaulted off the wall above the basin and landed undamaged on the floor.

"I had often found that mirror on the floor before, and this time I was so taken aback that I shouted out loud, 'Behave yourself. I am only going away for a couple of days!'

"Mine is one of four cottages that were built more than a century ago. I occasionally hear the sound of footsteps upstairs, and the previous occupant has told me that she sometimes felt an invisible presence brush past her on the stairs here.

"Despite this, it's a really welcoming and friendly cottage and I am never the slightest bit afraid of my ghost. I don't know if it moves the mirrors to get my attention – or because it doesn't like it when I go away," laughed Lesley.

HAUNTED COAL SCUTTLE

When a brass scuttle full of coal moved across the fireplace at her parents' cottage, Lorraine Davis could hardly believe her eyes.

"I was sitting on my own in the lounge in front of the fire one night in 1978, when I heard a grating noise and saw the coal scuttle move almost three feet across the flagstones on the hearth. When I told my dad what had happened he just laughed and said, 'Oh, it happens all the time, usually around nine o'clock at night'. He thought nothing of it."

Yvonne Davis and her late husband, Rodney, bought Tattles Cottage at Thorley near Yarmouth in 1975. Originally built as a farm cottage in the seventeenth century, it has been extended and modernised into a charming country home. "The place was falling to bits when we bought it - there was even a well under the lounge floor. We literally ripped the place apart then put it back together again, and my husband built us a fireplace from old Island stone," said Yvonne.

Soon after moving in the family realised the place might possibly be haunted. Lorraine's grandmother came to stay...just once. She never came again after encountering the ghostly figure of a woman wearing an old-fashioned bonnet, which she claimed was standing at the end of her bed.

This sighting was given more credibility when her next-door neighbour (in a house built in the 1970s) told Yvonne that she had seen a woman in a bonnet who cried and sobbed in a corner of her bedroom then disappeared through the wall.

Ghostly activity at the cottage peaked in the late 1970s when the family suffered metal hangers flying out of a wardrobe, the regular nightly thud and pattering sound of feet crossing a bedroom floor at 9.15pm, followed by a loud crash, which sounded as if an ironing board was falling over.

However, small items, usually jewellery or keys, still go missing for months on end. "They do turn up again, always in a place we have searched. I'm waiting for a gold charm bracelet to be returned at present," laughed Yvonne.

Whatever haunts her home may also be passing through a neighbouring cottage, formerly used as a holiday home. "We kept a key for it so we knew when it was occupied. However when the place was empty we heard the latch go up on several occasions, but whenever we checked, the house was always empty.

"We once asked the people who used to live here if the cottage was haunted. They looked at one another, and then admitted that 'something' used to shake the end of their son's bed. Fortunately we never had that happen," Yvonne said. "It may be haunted but there's certainly nothing unpleasant here. This cottage has a lovely warm and friendly feeling."

STEP BACK IN TIME

An American visitor saw more of quaint old Victorian England than she bargained for during a visit to the haunted former home of pioneer photographer, Julia Margaret Cameron.

It was noon on Sunday 13 July 2002, during a glorious spell of hot weather, when Kathie Boelkes visited Dimbola Lodge at Freshwater Bay. After first looking around downstairs at the books and postcards on sale in the hallway, she walked slowly up the old polished, wooden staircase to the galleries and exhibitions on the first floor.

Kathie recalled, "As I reached about the fifth step, the entire upstairs changed into a hallway that isn't there now. On the left was a man with white, thinning hair, who was in his sixties. To the right was a slender woman with brown hair. They just stood there looking at each other. Neither of the people noticed me.

"I knew immediately that they were not in my space or time - as the upstairs at Dimbola had somehow altered.... I felt that I was an observer in their dimension instead. However I wasn't at all afraid. They didn't react or speak and the scene before me lasted about four seconds before changing back to the present day."

Kathie said, "It was a remarkable experience that day, however spirits are not uncommon in my life. Both my mother and her mother before her have seen and heard things - and I seem to have inherited this ability too."

During her step backwards in time, it may be that Kathie somehow encountered Julia Margaret Cameron herself. This pioneer Victorian photographer made Dimbola Lodge her home from 1860 to 1875. It is now open to the public through a charitable trust which rescued the house from demolition, with help and sponsorship from Olympus Cameras and internationally-known photographers such as David Bailey and Koo Stark. The house is a landmark in photographic history, which today attracts visitors from all over the world, and much of the restoration work was supervised by Mrs Cameron herself!

Her ghost has been seen all over the building and a phantom smell which originates from the rear of the house when musical evenings are held at Dimbola, has been linked to the strong chemical, sodium thiosulphate, which Mrs Cameron used for developing and fixing her photographs. Her hands were stained black by these chemicals and she carried their distinctive odour around with her. (You can read more about haunted Dimbola Lodge in *Ghosts of the Isle of Wight Books 3 and 4*)

MOST HAUNTED ISLAND!

Visitors have written to me about strange experiences they have had here on the world's most haunted Island. Here are a couple of their tales:

While recovering from major surgery, during which she had had a 'Near Death Experience' in 1989, company director and mother-of-two, Dawn Smith, stayed at Whitecliff Bay, near Sandown, with her (now former) husband and their children. It is possible that this experience on the operating table had left Dawn in a more psychically receptive state, for during this time she had two encounters with ghosts just days apart.

She explained, "Returning after a day out we drove along a road lined by tall trees that met at the top forming a tunnel. It was a dull afternoon, but as we drove towards a right-hand bend, bright rays of light suddenly shone through the trees and we noticed a grey-haired gentleman with sideburns, in Victorian costume.

He was walking with a large dog, which wasn't on a lead, along the side of the road. Aged about sixty, and well-built with a portly stomach, he wore a tall top hat, a long jacket, waistcoat and pocket watch. He was dressed in autumn colours of browns, greens and gold.

"He was as aware of us as we were of him. As we watched, he just faded away – along with his dog and the beams of light. A little further along the road was a 'normal' man walking a terrier on a lead. My 'ex' stopped the car, looked at me and asked, 'Did you see what I saw'?"

Another night, Dawn saw a terrifying sight, which has haunted her ever since. "It was growing dark as we approached a crossroads where there was a small inn across the road. Beside a dirt track stood a wooden gallows, where I saw the body of a man hanging and swinging there in the wind."

Dawn closed her eyes. Surely she was dreaming. She opened them again, but the awful scene was still there, and a detail that made it even worse was that the corpse was hanging upside-down, suspended by the ankles – just like the hanged man on a Tarot card. One of his long, black leather boots lay crumpled on the ground below. "Horrified, I closed my eyes again. I never want to see another sight like that – I've never forgotten it and often wonder why on earth he was upside down, and if anyone else has ever seen that awful scene. Not knowing the Island very well, I have little idea where we were that night. When we went back to look in daylight, we couldn't find the place again."

STRANGE DREAMS AND TERRIBLE NIGHTMARES

Jean Moule and her husband Dave spent a week's holiday at a picturesque thatched stone cottage at Wellow in June 1995. However, from the very first night in the old smuggler's home, they both suffered very strange dreams and terrible nightmares from which they woke exhausted every morning.

The couple from Basildon, Essex, were also woken by loud voices at 4am when the portable television (a basic model with no timer facility) would come on full volume, although they had switched it off the previous night. They slept downstairs because the rooms upstairs felt cold, unfriendly and somehow 'wrong'.

"Although it was June and the temperature was in the 70s during the day, the place was so cold in the evenings that we lit the fire. We even used extra blankets because the bedroom was so chilly. Our dog kept staring at the wall in the dining room, and once as if someone had called him, he climbed a very steep staircase and ran from one end of the cottage to the other, as if he was chasing or playing with them.

"Sitting in the lounge we would see the ornamental chestnut roaster above the fireplace swinging on its own, and our dog would stare intently at this. It was a very spooky place. Even in the kitchen you felt you were being watched. Two days before we were due to leave, Dave felt someone very gently holding his wrist just as we were about to go to sleep. He woke me as he jerked his hand away sharply.

"Next morning he insisted, 'I think we should go home.' We left a day early and were relieved to go."

Cowes and its shipyards from the air, pictured in 1980

Chapter Nine

WORKING GHOSTS

In past centuries, shipbuilding was the very lifeblood of Cowes, and for almost two hundred years, one company dominated this industry. The name J. Samuel White & Company Limited stands out above all others in the town's maritime history. When Thomas White transferred his family shipbuilding business from Kent to the River Medina at East and West Cowes in the early 19th century, it was the start of an enterprise that became a world leader in designing and building merchant ships, naval ships and lifeboats.

With an unrivalled reputation for quality and workmanship, the company slogan was 'White's-built, Well-built!' Over that time, thousands of men worked in the sprawling Thetis, Medina and Falcon shipyards, for the Island's biggest single employer, J.S. White's of Cowes, as it was known locally. Many famous ships were designed and built by White's and during both world wars, the yards' output for the war effort was among the highest in the country.

But by 1965, with British shipbuilding in general decline, the Royal Navy ship HMS Arethusa was the last ship completed at J.S.White's - although the engine works continued building steam turbines and air conditioning units. An American company Elliott Turbomachinery Ltd. bought J.S.White's in 1972, but pulled out a decade later. At this point, the Island's County Council split the Medina Road site near the chain ferry at Cowes into small industrial units providing accommodation for a range of businesses. This became the Samuel White Industrial Estate, which was later sold to America's Cup challenger and businessman, Peter Harrison.

During the last war, shipyards were a key industrial target for enemy bombers and many of the buildings were hit in air raids. In 1942, on the night of May 4/5, some 150 bombers dropped their deadly cargo on East and West Cowes, killing 80 people and injuring many more as incendiary bombs started a series of huge fires. The Cowes-built Polish destroyer Blyskawica, undergoing a refit at White's, effectively saved the town by turning her guns on the Luftwaffe.

Today those massive, busy shipyards, which dominated both these towns and so many lives, have all but disappeared. However, the ghosts there live on...

NOBODY COULD EXPLAIN IT!

Peter Scott, who lives at Yarmouth, began his working life as a young apprentice in the East Cowes factory of Saunders Roe. By the late 1970s he was in charge of security and safety at the former J.S.White's shipyard, which was then owned by Elliott Turbomachinery Ltd. Many a night he was called out by puzzled security staff who complained that locked doors were unaccountably opening and closing in the oldest part of premises, fronting onto Medina Road in West Cowes.

The finance offices on the top floor were always locked at 6pm when staff left and security officers would check the door at two-hourly intervals through the night. Peter explained that the men would carry out several two-hour patrols during their 12-hour shift, turning keys in clocks as they went around the site, so that their movements could be checked. But on many nights, that finance office door was not only found to be unlocked, but wedged securely open with a heavy, lead loftsman's weight.

"The security chap would re-lock the door, pick up this weight and return it to its place on a shelf in the drawing office. Five times out of ten, when he went back two hours later to check the door, it would be open yet again and wedged with the same weight. I have experienced this

The old offices at the former J Samuel White's shipyard in West Cowes

myself," said Peter. "The regular security men just accepted it. They didn't talk about it much. It was just something that happened to every one of them working nights. Nobody could explain it.

"If you watched the door, nothing would happen. Believe me, we tried! Whatever was doing this knew its way around, because these lead weights - and there were several of them (used to hold down plans of aircraft and ship's frames) had come from the drawing office, which was down a flight of stairs, through three doors and along a 50ft passageway," Peter said.

In the centre of that drawing office at J.S.White's once stood a decorative, cast-iron, spiral staircase, which went up to a room where plans and blueprints were stored. Shortly after one of the new American owners spotted it, this classic piece of British industrial architecture disappeared one day. "It seemed that one of Elliott's directors had a better use for it, and so it went," said Peter sadly. "The hole in the ceiling was boarded over and, thereafter, the only way to reach the old print room was via the external fire escape, which didn't reach all the way to the ground.

"One morning, two years later in 1978, I had a call from security to say that the drawing office was flooding and the water seemed to be coming from that old, unused print room above. I had to climb the fire escape and struggle to unlock the only door to the room, which had clearly not been opened for quite some time.

"In the corner was an old, brown glazed sink. The plug was in the drain hole and the old brass tap fully turned on, so that the water was overflowing onto the floor. Elsewhere the floor was covered in a thick layer of dust, which was undisturbed. As I moved to turn off the tap, sunlight shone through the window and I could see two years' worth of unbroken cobwebs with their threads still twined around the tap. I thought it was really strange but dismissed it as 'one of those things'."

Peter turned the tap off firmly, pulled the plug from the sink and wrapped the chain around the pipe. Then he locked the door and went back down the fire escape. A year later the same thing happened. This time Peter took a maintenance man with him.

"Nobody had drawn the key to the room since I had it the previous year and the door was still securely locked. The plug was back in the sink, the tap was turned on and the water overflowing again. This time we not only turned the tap off, we cut the water supply and removed the whole section of pipe. We never had any trouble there again!"

This fire escape led to the locked room

Sadly, the American owners of Elliott Turbomachinery announced the Cowes factory was to close and a financial director arrived to finalise details. He installed himself in one of the rooms on the first floor, directly above the security office. However, he didn't stay long, Peter recalled.

"One evening this American was working late in his office when suddenly, his door was flung wide open, although there was nobody outside. He shut it again, thinking someone was playing tricks and sat down at his desk. The door flew open again. This time, the director marched downstairs and shouted at the security man, demanding to know what he was playing at.

"The security man replied that he had just returned from his rounds. They were the only two people in the building he insisted. The American ordered him to check the building again, which he did. Back in his office the financial director left the door wide open and returned to his paperwork. The door slammed shut. Several times he opened it and each time he sat down, the door would shut behind him."

When the security man returned from his next round, the furious American was waiting for him. Peter, as Head of Security, was urgently summoned from home.

"When I arrived, the security man - who I knew to be a steady and reliable chap - told me what had been happening. I said 'I'll sit tight here and see what happens'. He went off on his rounds while I waited in the security room. A couple of minutes later the American was back downstairs, ranting and raving. It had happened yet again! I radioed the security man to ask where he was. Then I told him to stay put and I rang the phone nearest to his location. He answered quickly, so I knew that he was several hundred yards away from the offices.

"I assured the American we were the only people in the locked building. Next, I used my master key and went into the drawing office, where I found a heavy, lead weight weighing three or four pounds, to wedge his office door wide open.

"I went back to the security office and waited. Minutes later I heard a terrific bang as the door slammed shut. The American came running downstairs, briefcase in hand and asked to be let out of the building. We never saw him there again," smiled Peter.

"A day or two later, questions were asked by another director, Ray Rack. When I told him what had happened that night, he looked at me for a while, then said, 'Actually, I do believe you. Some very strange things have happened to me when I have been in this building at night.' But he wouldn't say more."

A FRIENDLY SOUL

Finally, one of the ghosts at White's showed herself to Peter. Alone one night in the locked building, he was walking down the back stairs from the finance office to the first floor. He explained, "I had gone down three steps when I heard someone following me. I turned to see a lady there, walking down behind me. I was no more than two feet away from her, so close that I could hear the rustling of her long skirt as she moved.

"She had blonde or pale red hair pulled back off her face and wore a pale skirt and costume. She was around 5ft 6ins tall and aged in her twenties. She was aware of me, and strangely neither of us was afraid of the other. She seemed to be a friendly soul. We just accepted each other's presence and walked on down the stairs.

"When we reached the first floor landing I went to the right, she to the left. Then she suddenly disappeared. It was quite bizarre. I later discovered her ghost was well-known to some of the old boys who worked in the shipyard many years ago. She was said to be a sister or daughter of John Lee White, one of the last members of the family to be actively involved in the business."

A GHOST ON THE LINE

Reg Blake also knows the old shipyard - and its ghosts - well. After three years working for the American owners, he was, for some 20 years, site manager there for the Isle of Wight Council. Reg, who lives at nearby Moor Green Road, was often called out at all hours to look into odd happenings at the old Cowes yard.

Countless times over the years he heard those footsteps moving, sometimes running, along the corridor above the security office. "Thinking there was an intruder we would go up there and search the building. We never found anything," said Reg. "At certain places around the site when you were on night patrol, your torch would suddenly go out, although the batteries were all still OK. As you locked or unlocked doors, the torch would fail and wouldn't work again until you were clear of that part of the building. More often than not, this happened in the part where old Samuel White once lived. There you would get a feeling of being watched, the hairs on the back of your neck would rise and you would have a few shivers. There were more than a few 'cold spots' about the place. Also here, strangely, some nights we would notice the smell of cucumber, which can be quite unmistakable.

"During our rounds we would make 'security net' calls, phoning our opposite numbers in security at Plessey Radar in Northwood. Many a time the phone wouldn't work, and in those days before mobile phones, we would have to go to a public telephone box and ring in from there. This would usually spark a security alert and the police would arrive to check on us. However, whenever telephone engineers checked why the phone was dead, they could never find a fault. After a while they just put it down as 'Jasper the ghost on the line again'."

Even the patrolling guard dogs were affected by the unseen presence at J.S.White's and in some places would stop suddenly, then throw themselves against a wall, whimpering. "Even in the old, empty boat shops you would hear the sounds of people walking around. Security guards would go round together because they were too nervous to go on their own," claimed Reg. "They wouldn't admit it of course! And when the American owners came into the offices to make late night calls to the States, they would ask you to stay with them because they were afraid to be in there alone."

Late one night, Reg actually caught a glimpse of one of the shipyard ghosts. The figure, which wore a flat cap, a scarf knotted around his neck, and old-fashioned leather welding gaiters around his legs, was disappearing into the largest of the boat sheds. Reg called out, "Can I help you?" There came no response. The man continued walking into the deserted shed, vanishing into a brick wall.

Peter Hodgson and John Durrell run Med Tec, an engineering design business, in the first-floor former electrical drawing offices of the old shipyard, where wartime air raid shelters can still be seen beneath.

Both men who originally trained at J.Samuel White's, previously worked at premises in the former Admiralty Overseer's office, which adjoins the shipyard in Medina Road. There, too, late at night, John has heard footsteps walking in the empty building.

Since moving to their present offices, next to the River Medina and the chain ferry, he has become accustomed to hearing footsteps in the deserted yard. "You can hear people moving around at night, and the noise of someone coming up the staircase to the office. I always lock the door when I'm working here alone at night," admitted John.

THE FOREMAN'S GHOST

A number of men who worked at J.S.White's shipyards have tales to tell of ghosts there. Some are nothing more than an over-active imagination on night shift; tricks played by workmates; the rise and fall of the tide affecting floor timbers; or the metal frame of a factory shed expanding and contracting.

When John Oakley's father worked in the Falcon Yard, next to the chain ferry at East Cowes, one of the men under him asked to be taken off night shifts. He wouldn't say why, but when pressed, explained that he'd just seen a man wearing an old-fashioned bowler hat walk through a wall in front of him. The figure came towards him, walked past his workbench, and disappeared into the wall. When he described the man to workmates, they laughed. 'That was an old foreman who worked here years ago. Those foremen always wore bowlers,' he was told. Other workers later confided that over the years, they too, had seen this ghostly foreman roaming the factory.

John had his own odd experiences in the welding bay at the Medina Shipyard on the West Cowes side of the river. "I would often have the sensation of someone standing right behind me, close enough to touch me," he said. "A number of us felt it there. The hairs on the back of your neck would prickle and if you turned quickly, something would move behind you. A couple of times I actually glimpsed it reflected in my welding screen, but it disappeared before I could make out what it was."

In the early 1990s, Ian Dawkins of Gordon Road, Cowes, sometimes worked late into the night, helping at a friend's workshop in the old shipyard. "I was never nervous when I was working there on my own. However, one night I had something definitely playing tricks on me when I was alone, with the doors locked."

It was a chilly evening, so Ian placed an electric fan heater on the workbench and switched it on. He went across to another part of the workshop to fetch some tools, then returned to the bench. Feeling cold, he noticed the fan heater had stopped working. It had been switched off at the plug. "I thought someone was having a laugh - until I remembered I was in there, alone, with the door locked," said Ian.

Switching the heater on again, he returned to work. Later he went to make himself a coffee, but when he returned to the bench, the heater wasn't working. It was turned off at the mains. Wisely perhaps, Ian decided enough was enough. He locked up and went home, leaving the old shipyard to its ghosts.

SPIRITS AT SAUNDERS-ROE

Across the River Medina at East Cowes, strange stories are also told about ghostly goings-on in parts of the old Saunders Roe factory site – now owned by GKN. Kev Cooper who has worked as a maintenance engineer there since 1974, knows the various buildings well and has heard and seen the odd ghost there.

When Queen Victoria was at Osborne House, she was guarded by soldiers from her Royal Household Cavalry. The men were stationed in barracks on the seafront and their horses were stabled nearby in the appropriately named Maresfield Road, where in 1915 factory sheds were subsequently built for bi-plane aircraft production. Here in the lower

part of the old shed, brickwork arches which once formed part of the stables can still be seen.

By 2003, the Maresfield works were redundant. For almost 18 months, Kev worked to clear the building of the old machinery and fittings. "I was on my own clearing a store out at around

Remains of the old Household Cavalry stables can still be seen inside the factory building in Maresfield Road

2pm one April afternoon when I heard the sound of horses' hooves clip-clopping nearby. I looked out of the window but could see nothing in the road outside. The sound however, continued to move through the empty building and past me at a slow and steady pace.

"On another occasion when I was working in there with a mate, I saw a transparent dark shape which moved quickly through the empty factory. It was just one of the odd things that happen there in the old buildings," said Kev.

Adjacent to Osborne House, the Royal Stable Block, built in 1861, was an integral part of the estate. After the Queen's death, the Royal Naval College was based there from 1903 until it was closed in 1921. During the last war the buildings were commandeered by the Government to accommodate Saunders Roe and were used as design offices until 1987.

Long before the design offices vacated the premises, security officers were puzzled by 'something unseen' which regularly set off the sophisticated, invisible infra-red alarm beams that criss-crossed the office buildings at night. The area affected was always around the same corridor leading to the canteen.

Kev explained, "The sensors would detect somebody in the area who was apparently moving through the beams, but whoever it was remained invisible...until the night a disembodied face appeared high up at the window! The security guard ran to the door he had just come through, but found it was locked. His key wouldn't work and for almost 20 minutes he was trapped there, trying in vain to open the door. Suddenly, the key turned freely. He rushed outside to find no one there and further checks revealed no sign of disturbance to the ground below where the face had appeared. He wasn't keen to go around those offices on his own in the dark after that!" said Kev.

These old buildings at Osborne contain water towers

God's Providence House, St Thomas's Square, Newport, where plague spared the occupants in 1584, is pictured here in 1914, when the premises belonged to Glass and China Dealer, Walter Wells

Chapter Ten

PHANTOMS OF OLD NEWPORT TOWN

THE CAMERA SHY GHOST

It's rare for a ghost to be actually caught on camera – so for one to be found in a camera shop is even more extraordinary. Although the bright and modern Jessops photographic store in the heart of Newport is full of hi-tech equipment, the old building it occupies hides a darker secret.

While no ghost has actually been seen at 95 Upper St James' Street, whatever haunts the three-storey premises likes to make itself heard as it moves about upstairs, directly above the heads of staff and customers.

Dave Colman, who managed the successful Isle of Wight store from November 1996 until 2002, is still at a loss to explain the activities of Jessops' camera-shy ghost. Of course all old buildings have their own particular sounds – the creaking and settling of timbers; expansion and contraction in heat and cold; noise and vibrations from heavy traffic outside. But when the shop first opened, staff quickly became aware of something else - something which could not be explained so logically.

"We would hear footsteps overhead when we knew there was no one upstairs. This often happened on a Sunday when the shop was quiet and the film-processing machine, which makes rather a noise, wasn't running. It was definitely footsteps moving about on wooden floorboards; we heard them quite regularly, and despite searching the premises for an intruder, we found nothing. We examined the shop's security tapes to see if anyone had been upstairs, but found nothing!

"We also heard doors being opened and closed. They are actually heavy fire doors which open onto Scarrots Lane and couldn't have been moved in this way. One Sunday we heard a tremendous hammering and banging on doors downstairs. We thought at first that kids outside were messing around, but no one was there. It was so violent that we could see the heavy metal fire doors actually shaking, as though they were being pushed."

Although camera-shy, Jessops' ghostly presence is no weakling, as David explained, "I was alone upstairs one afternoon when I heard the sound of something heavy being dragged across the floor in one of the front rooms which overlooks the road. In there are four large skips full of catalogues, so heavy that two people are needed to move each one.

Moorman & Son's is now Jessops camera shop

"Thinking that one of the staff was in there I called out 'What are you doing? You should be downstairs. Who is looking after the shop?' I was about ten yards away from the room, so when there was no reply I ran in there. All four heavy skips had been dragged across the floor and arranged in a square in the centre of the room."

Dave is not ashamed to admit that he beat a hasty retreat back downstairs, where he asked a bewildered staff member if he had just been upstairs. "Of course not," came the reply. "Why? Did you need a hand? I heard you moving things round up there." Still puzzled, Dave examined the shop security tapes. These proved he had been alone upstairs – alone that is, but for the unseen presence, which didn't register on camera.

Kim Hulacka has also heard those footsteps pacing to and fro overhead, and she was present when the heavy fire doors were shaken so violently that they bulged. She and other staff have often noticed the 'unpredictable' nature of electrical systems in the place, with odd power surges, and the triggering of the alarm system in particular areas of the store. Of course there may be a perfectly innocent explanation, for Number 95 is an old building with an interesting past...

Over many years a number of businesses have come and gone here, at the corner of St James' Street and Scarrots Lane. Within living memory the narrow thoroughfare of Scarrots Lane ran red with the blood of slaughter. Here many of the town's abattoirs once stood.

Animals bought at the beast market in nearby St James' Square were led here and placed in stalls at the rear of the slaughterhouses. Little was wasted. Meat went to the butchers' shops, hides to the tanneries, while bones were boiled down for glue. In a nod towards respectability it was renamed Commercial Road, but the old name crept back and Scarrots Lane it remains today. As this ramshackle collection of dwellings, corn stores, stables, slaughterhouses, interspersed with rag and bone merchants, cattle dealers, farriers and undertakers grew up there, the squalor and filth was quite distasteful for the good people of Newport.

Records show that Joseph Johnson, cornfactor, rag merchant, bone boiler and marine store dealer, plied his trade at Number 95 from the 1840s until at least 1871. It was also a greengrocers before John Sheath & Co, corn merchants, moved from the adjacent property (now MacDonalds) to run a pet shop for some 15 years, until Jessops opened there in the late 1990's.

The most significant business to occupy 95 Upper St James' Street, which could explain those ghostly goings-on, was Moorman and Son's. A Royal Warrant read 'By Appointment to Her Late Majesty Queen Victoria, house-furnishers, cabinet-makers, upholsterers, and undertakers.'

Up on that third floor, in dusty rooms long unused is the original coffin maker's table. Nearby is the glass floor, which was swung open to lower the finished casket through. At the rear of the premises was a small Chapel of Rest opening onto Scarrots Lane (where the fire door is now). Here bodies could be delivered out of sight, and horse-drawn hearses would collect the newly-filled coffins for burial.

Despite this macabre history, there's nothing negative about Jessops' shop today. Its friendly, bright interior positively welcomes browsers and customers. But if you should hear footsteps overhead, don't worry; it's probably just that ghostly undertaker putting the finishing touches to another casket.

A YOUNG URCHIN

Just around the corner in Scarrots Lane, the spirit of a young urchin haunts Purple Dreams, a clothes shop run by Vanda and her daughter Kirby. Here, a scruffy black-haired little ragamuffin, aged about ten, has twice been seen peering down the stairs by Kirby.

"As soon as we opened the business we started to hear footsteps, as if children were running around upstairs. My young grandson, will giggle and chuckle at an unseen presence, while at night, our little ghost likes to play in the shop. Some mornings we come in to find things have been moved around and feathers from the colourful feather boas which we sell, are all over the floor!

"The first time Kirby saw our little ghost he was peering over the top of the stairs at her. He wore short, ragged trousers and a flat cap on his tousled mop of black hair. However Kirby was really spooked, because he didn't seem to have a face. She couldn't see his features, just a blankness there. The next time he appeared, she just saw his little face peering over the banisters at her. He occasionally startles customers by knocking on the changing room wall and, when people stand under the trapdoor which leads to the attic, he gently blows on the back of their neck. He doesn't bother anybody though and we are quite happy to have him around," she added.

Although Vanda doesn't know who the little ghost is, it's likely that he's a young stable-boy who may have worked and slept in the hay loft. The shop, which opened in 1999, fronts a quaint little flagstoned courtyard off Scarrots Lane in premises previously used as plumber's yard. A century earlier however, Victorian stables and a hayloft occupied the site, and when the area was excavated for the courtyard, the complete skeleton of a horse was found there. The Diva hairdressing salon nearby is also haunted (you can read this story in *Ghost Island*).

GOD'S PROVIDENCE

In the year of our Lord 1583, Death paid a visit to Newport. And it was a most fruitful visit. Over six short months, hundreds perished as the rat-borne plague raged through the Island's capital town. The number of dead was so great that it was impossible to convey them all to St Mary's Church at Carisbrooke for interment and a new burial ground was opened at Church Litten instead.

By May 1584, Death was satiated; the plague was all but over. Records show that "At Mr Tuttiot's house ceased the plage, and God, of his marcy, toke ye plage from the Towne to our great comfort.'

This house which stands in the shadow of St Thomas's Parish Church, said to be the only one in Newport in which no-one died, was henceforth called God's Providence House. The ancient building stands en-route to Church Litten, whose narrow arched gateway dating from Tudor times, was just wide enough for a horse-drawn hearse to pass through. The name Litten comes from the Saxon word "Lic-tun"; 'lic' meaning dead body, and 'tun' meaning plot of ground - literally the Town of the Dead.

Despite being partially rebuilt following a fire in 1701, God's Providence House is still one of the oldest properties in the town. Its elegant bow-fronted Georgian windows and a beautiful shell canopy over the main entrance are remnants of Newport's more graceful past and God's Providence House enjoys a Grade II* listing as a very important historic building.

Today, God's Providence House is a popular restaurant and busy tea-room

Early in the twentieth century the property became a restaurant, and today, God's Providence as it's known locally, is a popular restaurant and tearoom, specialising in delicious traditional home-cooked lunches, cakes and teas.

In June 2000, Janet and Bob Freemantle took over the business. "When the lady who sold it to me said, 'Do you know you have a ghost in this place?' I didn't really believe her," said Janet. However, as a former officer with London's Metropolitan Police Service, she wasn't particularly worried.

"Taking on an ancient and historic place like God's Providence House is a huge responsibility. It's part of the fabric of old Newport and has to be treated with respect. It is an extensive building with lots of nooks and crannies and some very old wooden panelling. Some of the flagstones in the entrance date back to 1583 and the thick, heavy oak front door is thought to be at least a century older than the main part of the house. There is a magnificent Jacobean oak staircase dating back to 1701, and the kitchens are now situated where the stables once stood," she added.

A visit to God's Providence is a step back in time, but whatever ghosts linger there are certainly gentle and benevolent. In one dining room, known as the 'gift room', the shade of a little girl has been seen.

Little is known about the ghostly child, but staff and visitors occasionally feel her light touch when they're in that room. Di Young, who has worked at the restaurant for many years, describes it as "A female touch – a light stroke from someone or something unseen which is standing very close to me," and housekeeper, Helen, has also felt the ghostly touch at odd times.

Janet remains open-minded about ghostly goings-on at God's Providence. "If there's a presence here it's a nice one," she said. "I am the most down to earth, rational person but the longer I am here the more I think there must be something in this. It's a wonderful old building with a very peaceful atmosphere. But curiously, although it's a rambling Georgian house and restaurant in the very centre of town, we have never ever had any rats or vermin here."

Does this absence of rats explain why the plague never reached here and why the lives of the good folk at God's Providence House were spared, more than four centuries ago?

GENTLE GHOST AT POLARS

The gentle ghost of an elderly lady dressed in grey appeared to care worker Dawn Blake when she was on duty at a Newport home for visually-impaired and elderly people. It was the mid-1970s and Dawn was working at what was then known as the Polars Home for the Blind, in Staplers Road, (now the privately-owned Polars Residential Home).

Dawn explained, "It was about 2am one morning and I was in an armchair at the foot of the main staircase, doing a crossword puzzle. A cat came in through the window and ran off upstairs. But half-way up it froze, then came shooting down again and ran out."

Wondering what had spooked the animal, Dawn looked up. There on the old wooden staircase stood a tall, slim elderly lady dressed in a long, grey slubbed-silk dress. On her hands were dainty lace gloves. Her soft, wavy hair was grey and she wore elegant drop-pearl earrings. The woman, who appeared quite solid, made no sound. "She stood with her hand on the banister and just smiled at me. Thinking I was going crazy, I shut my eyes and when I opened them again, she had gone. However, I wasn't at all frightened. The lady had such a lovely face and sweet smile that I felt quite calm in her presence," said Dawn.

"I never told a soul about what I had seen. I started to believe I had imagined it until one evening a few months later, when there was a problem with the fire alarms and another girl, Marie, came in to fire watch with me. As we were discussing our duties she suddenly said, 'You have seen her, haven't you?'

"I said, 'Who?'

"Marie replied, 'The lady in grey. You've seen her.' I

A gentle elderly ghost was seen here at Polars

nodded, and that was it. Neither of us mentioned the ghost again. I recall that Marie used to read palms, so perhaps she was psychic. I never spoke about it again until many years later, and I have never forgotten the lady in grey; she was such a kindly, benevolent presence."

The ghost has not been seen in recent years and manager of the Polars Residential Home, Mandy Minshull, is not aware of a presence there now. So who could the lady have been?

Built in the 1800s, Polars was for many years the home of the prominent Mew family, owners of the Royal Brewery in Newport and Kingston Manor at Chale. Alderman William Baron Mew lived at Polars with Frances, his wife, and when he died in 1887, businesses in the town closed, flags flew at half mast and more than 1,000 townsfolk attended his funeral at Fairlee Cemetery. Was the widowed Frances Mew a kindly, gentle lady who often wore a favourite grey silk dress? Perhaps.

GHOST GIRL AT ST CROSS

A boatyard seems a curious place to find ghosts, especially those of a young girl and a heavy smoker, whose spirits linger at the Odessa Shipyard at Newport Harbour on the Medina River.

Jim and Sarah Holdstock, who bought the boatyard in 1995, live in the adjacent St Cross Pier House, (formerly St Cross Cottage) built in 1840 on older foundations previously forming part of St Cross Priory estate. One of Newport's ancient religious foundations, the Priory was built in 1120 as a cell of the French Abbey of Tiron. Legend has it that during a fierce quarrel one brother cut the throat of a fellow monk, dropping the weapon onto a flagstone, which was stained forever with blood. As a penance the guilty monk tried every day to remove the stains, but they always returned. This flagstone was later incorporated into St Cross House. When this was pulled down in the 1880s, the stone was displayed in the window of an antique shop in Crocker Street. The stains could still clearly be seen. Sadly, no one knows where it is today.

Formerly a 'two-up two-down' dwelling, which once housed a family with 11 children, the cottage was enlarged in 1980, after lying semi-derelict for years. This extension was built over an old alleyway, which once led to a terrace of small dwellings known as Blackhouse Cottages. These tiny cottages, have now been demolished. One had just two rooms, and all faced the river. The backs of the buildings were coated with tar to help weatherproof them; hence the name, Blackhouse.

This area of Newport Harbour known as Little London, came into being in the seventeenth century. Extending from Town Quay to Blackhouse Lane, it was probably so named because of the large number of London-registered barges that moored and unloaded there. In 1830, a shipyard at Hurstake built and repaired vessels of up to 500 tons, while the local Newport Shipping Company ran cargo boats up and down the river.

On the opposite bank lies Fairlee Cemetery, which opened in 1853. A century ago, infant mortality was so high that some families buried more children than they raised. Many of their graves are now sadly unmarked, the headstones have fallen victim to time, neglect and vandals. Still visible, however, is a row of three little matching headstones belonging to children of the Shepard family. Hannah, their great-grand mother, was resident at St Cross Cottage until she

St Cross Pier House at Newport Harbour

died there in 1879. Hannah, who lived to see 12 children, 77 grandchildren and 74 great-grandchildren, is buried near the centre of the cemetery.

More than a century later, shortly after the Holdstock family moved in, Sarah saw the ghost of a little girl in her dining room. At first she thought it was one of her own daughters standing by the glass panelled door, but on closer inspection, she saw the child was a "blurry shadow" dressed in what appeared to be a long, calf-length dress. The girl looked to be aged around eight or nine.

"I never really saw her clearly enough to register her features, although I know she had dark hair. It was more of an impression of a child standing there. I glimpsed her a number of times, always in the same place and usually in the morning when I was on my own in the kitchen. She just seemed to be watching me."

Sarah did not tell anybody about the little ghost in case it frightened the children. However one day her eldest daughter, Laura, was at the dining table doing her homework, when she looked up to see a little girl sitting on a chair opposite, watching her intently. Then, before her eyes, the apparition vanished. Her dad, when he heard her story, thought she had imagined it. So when Jim laughingly told Sarah what had happened, he was astonished when she said, "Oh yes. That must be the same little girl I keep seeing!"

Significantly, Jess, the family's old Labrador dog, took to lying in the very spot where the apparition appeared in the dining room - where that alleyway once ran to the cottages. And, in the adjoining bathroom, also built on the same thoroughfare, the family regularly smells the distinct, pungent aroma of cigarette smoke. No one in the house is a smoker, but this unmistakeable odour is often at its strongest in the early hours of the morning, between 1am and 3am. The ghostly smoker puffs away largely unseen, but has been glimpsed once, by a young visitor sleeping on a sofa bed in the dining

Old Blackhouse Cottages now demolished

Ghostly footsteps pass this riverside cottage

room who woke in the early hours to see the ghost of a man looking at him. The next morning he complained that it was a weird house, adding he realised it wasn't Jim in the room, because this apparition was clean-shaven!

Other visitors have also experienced the ghostly smell. When the family went on holiday, leaving the house empty, a friend came in daily to feed the dogs. He was quite worried to smell cigarette smoke in what he knew was an empty property and checked windows and doors, fearing there had been a break-in. When Sarah and Jim returned they had to explain it was their resident, chain-smoking ghost that he had smelled.

When the family first moved into St Cross Pier House, another ghostly odour - that of ancient oil lamps - would waft around the kitchen. This hasn't manifested now for several years. However, when working in his office - also built on the site of that old alleyway - Jim sometimes hears a gate opening and glimpses a figure walking past, but there's never anyone there.

Recently, while getting into bed one night, he heard the sound of hob-nailed boots crunching across gravel outside the bedroom window. At first he didn't give it any thought ...until he realised the road is now tarmac. There's no gravel there!

FOOTSTEPS ON THE GRAVEL

What Jim and Sarah didn't realise is that neighbours Vera and George Smith have been hearing this for years. Vera, now in her eighties, was born in the pretty riverside cottage and has lived there all her life. Her father, Captain Walter Mew, worked on the riverboats, and he too, would hear those phantom footsteps. In fact, many members of Vera's family have heard them over the years - always around Christmas time and always at night.

The unseen presence walks the same route, past the back door of the cottage, along the flagstone path to the gate and on down the road past Jim and Sarah's house. "We never saw anything, but year after year we heard heavy footsteps on the path outside. We always listen out for them at Christmas time," said Vera.

More than thirty years ago, Kev Cooper of Elm Grove, Newport, also heard those footsteps when he worked at the nearby Motor Marine works. "Some evenings and late at night when it was quiet outside you would hear someone trudging down the road towards Blackhouse Quay. Crunching on gravel, the heavy footsteps would fade into the distance – but there was never anyone there…"

No one knows why this weary spirit continues to walk along the river. Nearby Dodnor can be an unlucky place for some, and the Curse of Dodnor has claimed a remarkable number of lives there over the centuries. (You can read these stories in *Ghost Island*).

A BLOOD-CURDLING SCREAM

A ghostly blood-curdling scream was actually recorded on tape at the High Street offices of a Newport insurance broker. Prominent local businessman Ted Sheath remembers the ghostly goings-on at County Insurance Brokers (now Vectis Insurance), which peaked in the early 1990s with mysterious footsteps, foul smells and a ghastly scream.

Now retired and living at Carisbrooke, Ted is still a director of the business, which moved into the three-storey building at 144a High Street in 1984. Often when working there alone late into the evening, he was puzzled to hear footsteps walking from the rear of the old building past his first floor office.

"It happened between 6pm and 7pm in the evening, more often in the winter when it was dark, than in the summer. The first few times I shot out to see who it was, because I thought I was working there alone. After a while it happened so often, that I almost ceased to notice it. This went on for several years. The footsteps, which I believe were a man's treads, were quite distinct, especially on the wooden staircase. They started in a small lavatory and washroom at the back of the building, moved along the corridor and then down the stairs to the ground floor, always following the same path and direction.

Lower Newport High Street in the late nineteenth century

Other staff working late also heard those phantom footsteps. One evening, Di Walsh and her colleague, Steven, fetched some fish and chips for dinner. As they washed up their plates in the tiny kitchen at just after 6pm, both heard heavy footsteps trudging down the stairs. "We raced to the staircase but it was empty and all the doors were locked. The footsteps were so loud it had sounded like someone was wearing heavy boots or clogs," said Di.

A Most Foul Stench!

One Monday morning in the winter of 1991, when Ted unlocked the front door to the office, he was greeted by a foul stench. "I thought immediately that we had a problem with the drains, but none of us could find where the smell was coming from. All the staff could smell it - it filled the office. The smell was terrible; like something was rotting and putrefying, but strangely and much to our relief, it vanished an hour later."

This respite was all too brief however, for next morning the awful smell was back as bad as ever when Ted arrived at the office. Again no cause was found and an hour later it went again. This happened three mornings running, and then stopped as suddenly as it had started. Early on Thursday morning however, Ted noticed that a heavy framed mirror in the washroom (which only he used) was standing in the toilet bowl. 'That's curious', he thought, for the window and door were shut. Ted replaced the mirror on top of the cistern and thought no more about it – until the following morning, when the same thing happened. This time he stood the mirror on the windowsill, daring it to move again. It didn't.

However, the strange chain of events which had been building during the week, culminated in a blood-curdling scream.

"At about 4.30pm that day - a Friday afternoon - I was downstairs at the back of the main office, directly below my washroom," said Ted. "Suddenly, Di Walsh, shot out of her office, asking urgently 'What is it, what's happened?'

"She'd heard a terrible scream which she thought came from the rear of the building upstairs, and ran to see who was in trouble. The girl who was franking the mail up there had the surprise of her life when Di ran in to ask if she was OK. Next we went into the back garden to check there, but all was quiet. I told her someone must have been fooling about. When she had heard that scream I was only a few feet away from her, yet I had heard nothing – nor had anyone else in the office. She had imagined it, we told her.

"However, as luck would have it, Di had been using her Dictaphone when she heard the scream. And what's more, when she played the tape back, there it was, recorded for us all to hear. I admit I was shocked. It was a long, desperate and chilling sound, which sent shivers down the spine. We played it back several times and everybody listened in amazement. It was so very loud, yet nobody else in the office had heard it when Di did!"

After that, some staff were reluctant to venture upstairs after dark. However, whatever had been slowly building during those few days, culminating in the scream, was over; even the footsteps stopped for a while. Today they are heard only very occasionally; the building is otherwise ghost-free.

Where is the recording of that scream now? Staff at the Cowes branch of the insurance brokers were agog to hear it, so Ted lent them the tape. They played it through several times, and then one of them managed to press the wrong button and erased it by mistake.

Ted was furious. "I was so cross. I really should have made a copy before I let the original go."

Di Walsh was also very annoyed when the recording was wiped. "I was so concerned about the scream that we informed the police, in case a woman had been attacked nearby. That tape might have been evidence if there had been a crime!" she insisted.

Lower Newport High Street, from an early nineteeth century engraving

"It was quite long, very loud and sharp, and seemed to be coming from immediately above in the back room upstairs. It was so chilling. I couldn't believe I was the only one to hear it. When I replayed the Dictaphone, the scream actually drowned my voice out. I handed it to Ted and said, 'Now do you believe me'?"

Whatever dark secret lies behind this strange pattern of haunting remains a mystery. Before Ted took the building over, both 144 and 144a High Street were the premises of the century-old drapery business of Albion Spanner. A hundred years earlier they housed the china, glass and earthenware establishment of Frederick Morgan and Co.

GOOD MORNING GHOSTS

In 1994, Di Walsh moved across the road to work for insurance broker Hill House Hammond. A former building at 27 High Street once housed 'Joseph Gentle, linen and woollen draper, purveyor of mantles, jackets, shawls, haberdashery, hosiery and family mourning clothing to the good townsfolk of Newport'. When Di worked there, however, insurance policies and claims had replaced those garments and mourning costumes. The ground floor was split into three office rooms, one of which, despite the heating, was always freezing cold.

"I never went into that room in the morning without saying 'Good morning ghosts' and wishing them 'Good evening' when I left for the night," confessed Di. "There was a tangible presence there at times. We never saw anything, but odd things did happen. Something would tug at your clothes as you were standing at the filing cabinets, and on at least three occasions in the kitchen, I have seen forks fly out of a mug they were in on the draining board and shoot across the room. I know this sounds bizarre, but it was only a mischievous presence there; nothing malicious at all."

However, Di wasn't so unconcerned the day she was kicked on the ankle by the office ghost. "I was walking through the middle office when I felt a hard shoe kick me. I was alone in the room and I know I didn't imagine it, because it was quite painful. Perhaps I had accidentally trodden on him or her first!" she said.

Ghostly activity in the premises ceased after renovation work there in 2001 when the offices were converted into an open-plan room. "I think the alterations must have really upset whoever was haunting the place, because the sense of presence and that chill in that side office vanished overnight."

THE ALMSHOUSE GHOST

Alms - relief given out of pity to the poor: a good or charitable deed.
Alms-house - a house endowed for the support and lodging of the poor.

Few people hurrying about their business in Newport notice a small row of single storey, red-brick houses at the top of the High Street. Known as the Upper Almshouses, these tiny dwellings built in 1875, replaced an earlier charitable property founded in 1650 by Mayor of Newport Stephen Marsh. These almshouses, which are still in the ownership of the Newport Parish Church, originally consisted of four, one-room tenements. Occupied by 'four poor widows' who would be chosen by the churchwardens of St Thomas's, each tenant received the princely sum of ten shillings (50p) a year from the charity of John Serle. It was apparently once a condition of the charity that these widows must always wear grey.

The Upper Almshouses in Newport High Street were re-built in 1875

Today, just two almshouses remain on the site and in one of these lives Avril Marshall, who moved to the Island in July 1999. Although tiny, her almshouse home is warm and cosy, with a sunny, rear courtyard garden for Scratch, her cat. Shortly after moving in, Avril realised her almshouse was already occupied by a nosy spirit.

On the first night in her new home, Avril was lying in bed when she heard a strange scraping noise. "It sounded just like someone was plastering the wall. I could clearly hear plaster being slapped on the wall and smoothed off. Then came a scratching at the bedroom door. I thought at first it was my cat, but as I listened I realised the cat was in the bedroom with me. When I opened the door, the hall was empty."

Avril has regularly heard the scratching sound on both the bedroom and kitchen doors since that first night. She senses that the ghostly animal is a cat, for she has felt it weaving about her ankles in the kitchen, and sometimes it even jumps onto her bed. She has also felt a number of 'cold spots' in the bathroom and living room. One day a friend, who didn't believe in ghosts, was in the bathroom when all Avril's shampoo and perfume bottles moved off a shelf in front of him. "There is no way they could have fallen from that shelf; they were deliberately lifted off and placed upright on the floor," Avril said.

In August 2003, she caught sight of whoever was sharing her house - and it certainly wasn't a 'poor widow'. "At about 2pm one afternoon, I was in the kitchen standing at the sink, looking through some sketches I had done, when I had a strong feeling that someone was behind me. I looked over my left shoulder, then shouted out in surprise, for a man was standing close behind me, peering over my shoulder at the sketches. For a moment I saw him there, but as I shouted out, he vanished. I think he was as surprised as I was. He was somewhere in his forties or fifties, with gingery-red hair. He had a long face, large eyes and was only about 5ft 3ins tall. I wasn't frightened by him, just very surprised."

Whoever the ghost is, he hasn't appeared since, although Avril senses him about her home. He's also a touch light-fingered, with a fondness for small trinkets and jewellery, especially earrings, which disappear and then turn up again days or weeks later. Jumpers also go missing from Avril's wardrobe. Sometimes they reappear – she found one in her lounge sideboard. Others have vanished, seemingly for good.

Other phenomena, which manifest in the old almshouse are phantom smells, which come and go at random. Perhaps her ghostly lodger is bringing gifts, because lucky Avril sometimes notices a very strong smell of chocolate in the hallway and bedroom. At other times there's a sweet floral perfume in the bedroom. "It's a very distinctive fragrance, similar to hyacinths, and it happens at night when I'm in bed. Sometimes it's so overpowering that I get up, make a pot of tea, and sit in the kitchen until it has gone!"

A PHANTOM PRINTER?

Since the Island Olive Company opened a new Costa Coffee shop at 53 Pyle Street, in March 2004, the building's resident ghosts have taken a keen interest in the new enterprise. Staff are convinced there's a pair of ghosts in the building, and believe them to be an elderly man and a young boy.

Linnie Dykes has sensed the man's presence all over the building, but most especially in the first floor kitchen. "You can feel him moving around with you. Some mornings I have been aware of him coming downstairs with me. I feel he is interested and wants to know what we

Pyle Street, Newport, seen from the direction of St Thomas's Square in the 1970s

are doing here. Although I don't see him, I have an intuition that he's an elderly man wearing a long coat or apron down to his ankles. Two young girls who work here have complained that 'someone' is watching them and one was quite upset by it.

"I sense the boy, who I think is called John, is about ten years old and may have been apprenticed to a shopkeeper here. I don't know how I know this. It just popped into my mind," said Linnie. "I was sitting on the stairs one day during a staff meeting when I felt him poke my arm hard with a finger. I spun round quickly, but there was nobody there.

"One afternoon I found the freezer door open, although I know it was firmly shut when I checked earlier. I just knew he had done it so I challenged him, saying, 'There's a cherry tomato on the floor over there. Let's see if you can move it!'

"The tomato just sat there, but an hour later I found the freezer door open again. There was defrost water all over the floor, and the freezer temperature had risen from minus 18 degrees to plus 5 degrees, which, in such a short time was impossible. The ghost had certainly risen to the challenge and entered into the spirit of things!"

The man's presence feels strongest in two small, empty storerooms on the top floor. One day, when Linnie and two other staff members went upstairs, they encountered a strange pressure like an energy wave or a feeling of resistance on the third and fourth step, trying to push them back. When they finally reached the storeroom, the door closed suddenly behind them.

Feeling brave, Linnie opened it again and said out loud, 'Let's see you do it again then'. The door slammed shut. "The next day when I took my husband, who is a complete sceptic, very level-headed and grounded, up there, the same thing happened. Three times. He examined the door, the walls, looked for draughts of air and even jumped up and down on the floorboards. There was no way he could make the door shut in the same way."

Another staff member, Donna Froment, has also noticed the man's presence following her around the building. "I have felt someone watching me in the kitchen, and also moving down the stairs right behind me," she said.

Heidi Panayiotou who runs the Island Olive Company with Julian, her husband, said, "When we first looked around the building I felt comfortable everywhere, apart from the attic rooms. I do get the impression of a presence at times, particularly near a large mirror in the shop, where I glimpse someone moving, out of the corner of my eye."

The Ghosts Party

Whoever the ghosts may be, they're not particularly tidy, for on Monday 31 May, 2004, a Bank Holiday morning, Linnie and Heidi arrived early at the premises to find they were still securely locked, but in rather a mess.

Biscuit and cake crumbs lay on the tables and floor, while behind the chill-counter, coffee grounds had been scattered about the floor. Coffee drips had been sprayed on cupboard doors and behind the counter a man's medium sized footprints could be seen.

"The place was spotless when we left. We had cleaned thoroughly before leaving on Saturday evening. I can't imagine how it got into such a state. It was as if there had been a party," said Heidi. "If so, the ghosts must have really enjoyed themselves!"

Interestingly, this area of Pyle Street has long been haunted. Until 1995, Hazard's shoe shop was next door at number 94. Here, a sensation of cold and the pungent whiff of cigar smoke were noticed by customers and staff. The shoe shop has now been incorporated into the bank premises, which stand on the corner of St James' Square.

During building work, staff at a hair salon and fashion shop at 53 Pyle Street, which is now the Island Olive Company, noticed that a ghost had suddenly become active there. Unseen hands set a huge chandelier swinging above the staircase. A 'presence' would brush past staff, who also complained that they were being watched and could hear heavy footsteps moving around. A

The Isle of Wight County Press

THE
ISLE of WIGHT
NEWSPAPER
is the
"COUNTY
PRESS,"

Published
SATURDAY
MORNING,

Price 1d.,

In every Town
and Village.

Containing complete
compendium of
Island Intelligence
and Summary of
General News.

In November 1884 the Isle of Wight County Press was first published here, and cost one old penny a week

not dissimilar pattern to the current ghostly activity there! Research has shown that early in the last century, 53 Pyle Street was a print shop for Mr J Howard Burgess. In Victorian times, yet another printer and bookbinder, Thomas Kentfield occupied the premises. Immediately next door 'in commodious premises on the corner of St James' Square' the Isle of Wight County Press newspaper was first produced in November 1884, before moving into purpose-built High Street offices and works almost 30 years later. Perhaps, if Linnie's intuition is correct, the ghosts at 53 Pyle Street may actually be the earthbound spirits of an elderly printer, dressed in a long coat and printer's apron, and John, his young apprentice.

THE DISAPPROVING SPIRIT

An elderly ghost who couldn't abide television when he was alive, switched off programmes he disapproved of in a neighbouring house after he had passed away. Pauline and Clive Burt have lived at their three-storey terraced house in Chapel Street, Newport, since 1972. But it wasn't until their elderly neighbour died unexpectedly in the late 1990s, that odd things began to happen.

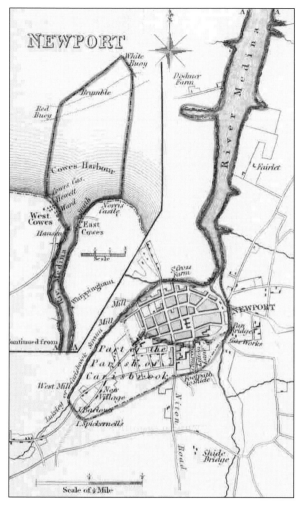

An early map of Newport and Carisbrooke

"We would have our TV on in the front room and whenever anything a bit loud, exciting or sexy came on, the set would be instantly switched off. It was quite bizarre. It wasn't a fault in the set; for the TV was physically switched off each time. When we realised what was happening, we just had to laugh. Our neighbour George, who was a quiet man, had always hated television and would never have it in his house. After he died his house was sold, so I think he came to visit us instead," Pauline said.

"At this time we kept dachshunds, and our dogs could always sense when George was around, because they would stare at the living room door and growl.

"One night when I came home from work, the dogs were barking. I went indoors and as I reached the bottom of the stairs I froze. I could sense 'something' there with me. Then I felt someone blow into my ear. It felt really cold. I turned and although the hall was empty I said 'George, I am surprised at you. I didn't think you were like that!'

"Occasionally we would hear footsteps in the hall and the sound of stairs creaking as someone went up. Our new neighbours, two police

The changing face of old Newport can be seen in this photograph taken in 1984

officers, also heard someone moving about their house and told us other weird things were happening there. This went on intermittently for three or four years, then gradually tailed off.

"There is still an occasional burst of ghostly activity – my daughter was upstairs cleaning her teeth one night when she came downstairs looking deathly pale. She was so convinced she had heard someone go upstairs into the attic bedroom that her father went to check. Clive came back downstairs with his hair standing on end. He had gone into that room only to find it empty, but freezing cold.

"Although he's mostly quiet now, we still talk to George, and our new dog, a German Shepherd, sometimes senses him around. Apart from interfering with the television, George rarely moves anything. However, one night we were sitting in the front room when a framed photograph of our son, which was hanging on the wall, suddenly peeled open. The frame seemed to come apart although the glass stayed in and the photo fell to the floor. It was impossible. We just looked at one another and said 'Did that really happen?'

"It has never really bothered us having George around, he was such a gentle soul when he was alive that he's not going to frighten us now he's dead. I think he was probably a bit lonely in his old house and just came to us for a bit of company. It's just a pity he's not keen on our choice of television programmes," Pauline added.

ROCK COTTAGE LADY

The elegant figure of a ghostly woman wearing a long dress and hat has been seen walking across the garden of a 350-year-old stone cottage, which stands on the approach to Carisbrooke Castle. Although Rock Cottage in Castle Road was originally built in 1650, the ghost has only been seen in the rear courtyard garden, which along with the kitchen, is a more recent Victorian addition.

When architect Harry Wheeler, partner Kate and children Tom, Rosie and May, moved into the property, one of the oldest in the village, in June 2002, they had no idea that it was haunted. Whoever the elegant ghostly lady is, she quickly made herself noticed by switching electrical appliances such as hair curlers, mobile phone chargers and boiler timers, off and on. The family then found light bulbs were being removed from kitchen sockets and placed, carefully, in the sink.

Several times in the early hours, usually at around 4am, unseen hands have opened Tom's bedroom door wide. At other times, usually in the evening, the sound of a woman's footsteps can be heard walking through the hall from the front door. A recent visitor to Rock Cottage, who told Kate she had grown up there, confirmed that those footsteps had also been a regular occurrence when she lived in the house.

One September evening at about 7pm, young May, then aged six, piped up, "Mummy, I just saw a lady with a long dress and hat on walking across our garden and back."

"She wasn't worried or frightened," said Harry. "She just wondered who the lady was! Actually, although neither Kate nor I have seen her, we have had the impression of a grey figure in the garden. Certainly whatever is here feels benign and friendly, and in a cottage this old, it would be almost disappointing if we didn't have a ghost."

Many soldiers were garrisoned at Carisbrooke and Newport over the centuries and it's said that their ghosts have been seen and heard in Castle Road - which is the main approach to the castle.

One of the oldest properties there, Rock Cottage was built just after the unfortunate King Charles I failed in his bid to escape from Carisbrooke Castle and was subsequently beheaded in 1649. "It has long been rumoured that a tunnel exists between the castle and Rock Cottage," said Kate. "We haven't found it yet, although there's a deep well in our garden which may possibly be hiding something."

Built in 1650, Rock Cottage is haunted by a woman's gentle ghost

Chapter Eleven

SPIRITS OF THE NORTH

'ONE OF *THEM* IS HERE AGAIN'

From the first moment she set eyes on her cottage, more than twenty years before she bought it, Mary Wright just knew it was the one for her. "Shortly after I had just met my husband and we were out for a drive, I saw the house and immediately wanted to live here," she said.

As luck would have it, some years later as a district nurse at Cowes in 1981, it was Mary's job to call, two or three times a week, on the elderly couple who lived in her dream home in Pallance Lane at Northwood. Both had suffered strokes and as they were unable to manage the stairs, they lived and slept in the front lounge. One day, Mary arrived to find the old lady shuffling around the house on her walking frame, saying her prayers as she went. "What on earth are you doing, Doris?" she asked.

"One of them is here again," she replied, but refused to explain what she meant, so Mary smiled, dismissing the incident as an 'elderly moment'. Two years later her patients moved into a residential home, and they offered Mary first refusal on their house. She jumped at the chance, and by June the family had moved in.

"The house had a wonderful welcoming atmosphere and I still love it as much today as when I first saw it," said Mary. "However, we soon became aware that we were sharing it with an unseen presence. Our youngest son, Dan, then aged six, arrived in our bedroom one night to ask why I kept shaking him awake. I thought he'd been dreaming and sent him back to bed - but a few nights later it happened to me!

"Our eldest son, then 13, was not comfortable when he was there alone and would insist on switching every light in the house on. One day I was out in the stables at the end of the garden when I heard my husband, Don, shouting for me to come immediately. He had been upstairs, fitting a cupboard in the bathroom, when he felt a pair of invisible hands on his waist moving him aside."

Then the smells started. Just before Christmas the fragrance was amazing; a mixture of floral scents like an old English rose garden, which would waft around downstairs. Sometimes Mary would wake at night to the delicious smell of bacon and eggs frying. The aroma, which was confined to the bedroom, was sometimes powerful enough to rouse her from sleep. Then it would disappear suddenly, as if switched off.

Next, the footsteps started. They could clearly be heard walking up the stairs and into the bathroom. When Mary told a friend who had known the previous owners, she remarked, "It's happening just like before." She also told Mary that although the elderly couple had been unable to use the stairs, their brush and comb would frequently be found upstairs in the bathroom and the immersion heater there would be switched off. Mary's cats and her elderly dog, Edward, would often sit at the foot of the stairs staring intently, as though watching something.

One night Mary came face to face with a figure leaning over her bed. "I had been on the mainland at a pony show and was so tired that I went to bed early. But in the early hours something woke me. I opened my eyes to see an old lady peering down at me. I told myself I was still asleep and dreaming. But I opened my eyes again and she was still there. I flung both my arms up and jumped out of bed. I was so scared that I actually threw up. For the rest of the night I lay awake with the light on."

Beady Black Eyes

The solid-looking figure Mary saw was that of an elderly woman with beady black eyes and a wrinkled face. Her long, grey straggly hair was tied back with a coloured band and her clothing was a patchwork of different fabrics, with many mends and darns in it.

In the cold light of day, Mary realised it was just the shock of seeing the ghostly figure which had caused her to have such an extreme reaction. However, she was concerned enough to call in a local clergyman to cleanse and bless the family home. Since that time the footsteps have stopped and the old lady has not visited again.

However, the smells of sweet flowers downstairs and mouth-watering fry-ups upstairs continue to tantalize the family. Now they also have to keep an eye on their telephone directory, which regularly vanishes for days on end. "Quite why a ghost should need a phone book, I don't know," laughed Mary. "It's always kept in the same place in the dining room, but on countless occasions it has disappeared, apparently into thin air. At first we would almost tear the house apart searching for it. Now we know better. It will come back eventually. Keys, too, will disappear for weeks at a time. You can put them down and moments later they're gone. We also have problems with the hot water tap in the bathroom being turned on - usually when we are all out. And we sometimes see a figure walking past the kitchen window to the back door. We are so certain a visitor has arrived that we open the door, but there's never anyone there."

Don added, "Actually this area of Pallance and Luton Lane, the little unmade lane nearby which leads to the Luton Farm, is rather peculiar. Some nights I take the dog for a walk there and it feels fine, but at other times there is a sensation of menace so strong that I won't go that way. Other people here have told me they also experience that same intangible but distinct feeling that they should avoid the lane."

The cottage is one of a pair of farm labourer's dwellings built in the late 1800s, as part of the Luton Farm Estate, which appears in records as far back as 1086. One day Mary bumped into an old acquaintance who asked her where she lived now. When she told him, he laughed and said his great-grandmother, a gipsy woman, had once lived in her caravan in the field opposite! So, was it the ghost of an old tinker woman which Mary saw that night? Curious to find out if this was true, Mary discovered that the old name for Pallance Road was Tinkers Lane – so called because of the gipsies (tinkers) who once lived in the area.

PHANTOM AT THE PARSONAGE

At the end of Luton Lane stands the old Northwood Rectory, now renamed Tara House (by a former owner who was a fan of Gone With the Wind). Here, Liz Mackenzie, her partner and daughter Georgina, live in the rambling, haunted, early Georgian house, which they are slowly renovating.

Liz bought the former rectory at auction in 1987, just a month before a hurricane blew most of the roof off, demolishing a wall and several windows. "The house was in a terrible state of decay. There was only gaslight when I bought it and many of the floorboards and joists downstairs were rotted or missing. There was an oak tree growing in the drawing room with its roots coming up through the dining room floor!"

At one time the house was the rectory for a parish covering both Northwood and Cowes. Reverend Thomas Troughear who re-built the property in 1736 was also Vicar of Carisbrooke. He married well, to a granddaughter of Governor of the Island, Admiral Sir Robert Holmes. His eldest son Leonard, a Member of Parliament for the Island, inherited the title and the grand house of Westover at Calbourne.

Now Tara House, this was once a Rectory

However, by Victorian times, Rector of Northwood, Reverend Shadrach Seaman, was reduced to supplementing his stipend by educating 'sons of gentlemen for public schools and the universities'.

The Church authorities sold the old rectory in the 1950s when a new one was built in Chawton Lane, closer to the twelfth-century Northwood Parish Church. The lady who bought it, eventually died there in her nineties, as the house decayed around her. When it passed to Liz, she used the property as a holiday home for several years while doing the renovation work. Now the family live there permanently.

"I knew from the first that the old rectory was haunted," said Liz. "James Jones, the surveyor who checked the property for me actually wrote in his report that it came with a ghost! Since then, we have glimpsed a ghostly woman's figure about the place at odd times.

"Recently as I was coming down the attic stairs, I saw a woman in a full-skirted long dress at the foot of the staircase near my daughter's bedroom door. I don't believe in ghosts but I was quite shocked to see this solid, dark figure standing only two or three feet away. She started to move towards me, then vanished."

Since moving to the former rectory, young Georgina has started talking to an imaginary friend named Connie. "This began when she was three and she is always chatting to 'my friend Connie' who apparently lives here with us. We don't make an issue of it, however, I sometimes wonder if Connie is the name of our ghostly lady," said Liz.

VINTAGE GHOST CAR

Is it possible that a visitor to the Island saw the lights of a ghostly car chasing him down a lonely country road, one August night?

Builder John Miles of Waltham Abbey has spent his holidays on the Island every year since 1963, when, at the age of 11, he first came here with his family. Between 1994 and 2000 he always stayed at Thorness

Bay Holiday Park near Cowes, so is familiar with the local lanes and back roads there, having travelled them many times by day and night.

"My experience happened on Thursday, 10 August 2000. At about 10.45pm, I was returning from Lake with my girlfriend's six-year-old lad who was chattering away at my side. I drove along Forest Road and turned into Whitehouse Road. The roads were unusually quiet and there had been no other vehicles on the road until then. Suddenly, in my rear view mirror I noticed faint car lights, which were catching up with me. I was only travelling at about 30mph because that road is in a bad way!

"I could just make out a vintage car with a long bonnet and huge chrome headlamps. At first I thought it was only showing sidelights, but then I realised these were the dim headlights of this old vehicle, which didn't cast any light onto the road. Despite its age it was approaching fast. I decided to speed up as I had a straight stretch of empty road in front of me, but I couldn't throw off the old car, which remained almost stuck to my rear bumper. I started to feel frightened because I sensed something here was very wrong. By this time we were doing 50-60mph and the car was still right up behind me. I couldn't see a driver or even make out a number plate.

"At this point I realised that although I had my windows open on that August night, I could only hear my own car's engine; the vehicle behind was silent. I started to panic. Then, to my great relief, I saw a car approaching from the Cowes direction. As it passed me, I looked again in my mirror. All I could see were the vanishing tail-lights of the other vehicle. The old car had disappeared! But there was nowhere it could have gone. There were hedges on both sides and no turning it could have taken (it could also not have made a turn at that speed).

"I have never believed in ghosts but I can't explain what happened that night. I would love to know why the old car appeared and if anyone else has seen it. I know I didn't imagine it, but I cannot come up with any rational explanation for the weird events that night," said John. "I tend to use the main roads at night now when I visit the Island," he added.

THE AIRMAN'S LONELY SPIRIT

This poignant little story from Roger Williams concerns his late aunt, Esther Twyman, who taught at Northwood School for many years. "At one time my aunt and uncle lived in Place Road at Cowes. My Uncle Stanley, a semi-invalid with heart trouble was unwell so Aunt Esther was sleeping downstairs. One night she went to check on him and as she climbed upstairs she saw the ghost of a young airman in uniform, standing on the staircase, wearing his 'Mae West' lifejacket.

"As my aunt walked towards him, the solid-seeming figure simply disappeared. My aunt wasn't afraid, but she was very curious, so set about discovering why the ghostly airman was haunting her house. After making inquiries locally, she learned that the daughter of the previous owners of the house had been engaged to marry a pilot. Tragically, his plane was shot down and he was killed in the early years of World War II.

"Several months later, the phantom airman appeared again, still wearing his life jacket. This time Aunt Esther was ready for him and she said, 'I am very sorry but your young lady does not live here any more. She has gone away'. At that the airman's ghost disappeared through the wall. He never returned."

PHANTOMS AT PARKHURST

After working at Camphill Prison during the summer of 2003, Russell Chantler was transferred on a temporary contract to neighbouring Parkhurst Prison in November that year. "On my first day at Parkhurst, as I entered the prison I noticed a hugely oppressive atmosphere. I'd been at Camp Hill for several months, so I was used to working within a prison, but this felt different. As I got to know the place, I found parts of the prison very oppressive to be in and around, especially the older buildings. I felt uneasy in non-populated areas of the prison on my own - as if I was being watched, even though I was working within areas that weren't used much, such as roof spaces of the wings and in the cellars.

"I'd heard through colleagues, about ghostly sightings and happenings, but didn't take them seriously. Until one particular day when I escorted a building contractor to a roof space in the wing which was badly damaged during prison riots some years ago. It was a huge area, and very warm up there. The builder went back downstairs to fetch something. The door was locked behind him and I was left there to keep an eye on his tools.

"Suddenly I became aware of a penetrating coldness around me. I was wearing a short-sleeved shirt because the roof space was so hot and stuffy. Then I felt a tickling on the top of my head as I knelt to tie up my bootlace. Brushing away what I thought was cobwebs; I continued to tighten my boots. However, the tickling continued. Goose bumps appeared on my arms, then I felt someone poking me in the back with their finger. It was a very real sensation. I knew nobody else was within the area as I had the keys to the only door, which was locked. It was at this point I gave up and went back downstairs. I chose not to say anything to my colleagues for fear of being ridiculed, but for the rest of my contract at Parkhurst, I avoided the area where I worked that day."(Read more about the haunted prison in *Ghosts of the IW Book III*)

'YOU WEREN'T ALONE THERE'

Until they moved to Cowes at the start of the new Millennium, the Island's library headquarters were sited across the main road from the Parkhurst, Albany and Camp Hill gaol complex. Originally built as Parkhurst Barracks in 1799, it was re-named in honour of the Duke of Albany, the Commander in Chief of the British Army. The site once extended over 150 acres and included a large military hospital and orphan school for soldiers' children. Later it was used as a depot for troops bound for service abroad, because 'this insular situation is found more convenient than Chatham for preventing desertion'.

Here, in one of the old buildings which once formed part of Albany Barracks, Phil Cotton worked for 13 years as a display technician for Isle of Wight Council. This vast, two-storey brick building known as the 'Tank Bay' was formerly used as a tank repair workshop by the Army.

"It was a strange place to work in," said Phil. "You could always feel an unseen presence there. Even when you thought you were alone, you never were. When I was on my own with the door locked, I would still hear footsteps upstairs. There were other noises overhead, too. Bangs, thuds and the sound of something heavy being dropped. It was not a nice place to work. You could never get warm and certain areas of the workshop felt bone-chillingly cold, even on the warmest summer day," added Phil.

Perhaps that's why the old building, which is close to St Mary's Hospital, was chosen as a temporary mortuary and apparently used to store the remains of some of those killed in the Island's worst-ever air disaster. This happened in 1957 when a Short Solent flying boat owned by Aquila Airways, en-route to Madeira via Lisbon, crashed shortly after take-off from Southampton and burst into flames in a chalk pit at Chessell, near Yarmouth, killing 45 people.

The bodies of other unfortunate victims were taken to the old officers' quarters at Golden Hill Fort, Freshwater, which also served as a temporary mortuary. Among the dead was a concert pianist, whose spirit lingered for many years afterwards in the

The haunted former 'Tank Bay' at Parkhurst

empty building, where the sound of a piano could be heard as he gave a final concert from beyond the grave. (You can read more of this story in *More Ghosts of the Isle of Wight.*)

SPIRIT OF BEATRICE AVENUE

If you travel at night along Beatrice Avenue at Whippingham, watch out for an elderly man who walks with his little dog along the lane, towards East Cowes. He's between 65 and 70 years old, wears an old, flat cap, and is accompanied by an elderly terrier on a lead. Nothing out of the ordinary here you may say, but they are actually apparitions that have been seen in this quiet lane by several people, including local builder, Kevin Burch, of Vectis Road.

A few years ago, Kevin and his family would regularly use what's known locally as the 'back road' when they cycled home after visiting his mother in Ryde. "We would often see the old chap, who was always walking in the same direction, from St. Mildred's Church towards East Cowes. We would come up behind him and ride past. But if we looked back, he would have vanished.

"This happened countless times. In those days there were no breaks in the hedge, or turnings he could have stepped into. He simply disappeared. It was always around the same time of night, between 9.30pm and 10pm, and it happened the same way every time. It was so spooky that we stopped using the 'back road' and cycled home on the main road instead," said Kevin.

Chapter Twelve

SPOOKS, SPIRITS AND HAUNTED INNS

In 1992 I wrote a strange, intriguing story about 'The Pub That Wasn't There'. This mysterious inn, somewhere between Newtown and Calbourne, has never been seen again since that dark November night in 1982, when two Island friends dropped in for a drink. Many readers are fascinated by this tale and more than a few have tried to find it for themselves. I suppose a ghost-pub crawl is a good way to spend an evening and come home sober!

When Laurie West originally contacted me about his encounter that night, it wasn't with the intention of having his story printed (in fact he was most reluctant to do so) it was to find out if anyone else had reported a similar experience. Nobody had - until now. (Read Laurie's account of The Pub that Vanished in *More Ghosts of the Isle of Wight*).

Once again this new story came to me in a roundabout way, via a friend of a friend. I wasn't approached directly; in fact Wendy and Gary Lacey were initially surprised and dismayed that I wanted to ask them about it. However, they finally agreed to meet me and for almost two hours we talked, going over their account in exhaustive detail. It bears certain similarities to Laurie's story, but there are many essential differences, as you will see.

ANOTHER PUB VANISHES

It was early one summer's evening in 1990 and the couple who now live at Hazel Close in Upper Ventnor, had just dropped their young son Robert off at Corfe Scout Camp near Newtown. The weather was fine so they drove back via Yarmouth, where they intended to have a meal. However they were too early and the restaurants weren't yet open.

"We continued out of Yarmouth, past Chessell and Brook, towards Shorwell. Somewhere, between Brook and Brighstone, at between 5pm and 6pm we stopped off at a pub. It was similar to but was definitely not, the Sun Inn at Hulverstone. The two-storey stone building, which had a slate roof, was decorated with a string of old-fashioned electric light bulbs, and there was an empty gravelled area at the side, where Gary parked our old Metro.

"From where we left the car we could see fields and the Downs. We could hear birds singing, for remarkably, there was no traffic passing on the road. It was a strange place," said Wendy. "Gary who works as a postman has lived on the Isle of Wight all his life, and I've grown up here too. We both know our way around the Island pretty well – and where all the pubs are! However, this was not one we had ever seen before. We stood outside, in two minds whether or not to go in. Then Gary said, 'Let's go for it,' and we pushed the front door open and stepped inside.

"We went down two or three steps into the bar, where there was an old-fashioned, dark wooden rail with banisters and a wooden top. The room was quite big and although the evening was warm, it was chilly indoors. We stepped up to the wooden bar. Serving behind it was a middle-aged man in an old blue-checked shirt. He wore his baggy trousers high on his waist, held in place by a belt. The woman with him - presumably his wife - wore a full-length 'pinny' style apron in a faded, old-fashioned floral pattern.

"I asked for a glass of wine. 'We don't sell that here,' said the landlord. So I had a glass of cider instead. Gary asked for a pint of beer and a packet of crisps, but there were no crisps; in fact the pub didn't have a menu or serve food at all. There were only a few dusty bottles behind the bar, which appeared to be very sparsely stocked. Gary paid for the drinks and immediately pocketed the change. But the money was 'wrong'; there were old pennies in it - although we didn't notice this until we were back in the car.

"A few men were sitting at the bar and, as the only woman standing at the bar, I felt their hostility, as if I shouldn't be there. I felt like an alien and was so uncomfortable that we took our drinks and went to sit at one of the old, varnished tables instead. There was only one room as far as we could see, with horrible worn, blue linoleum on the floor. Everything looked old and shabby. It's difficult to explain, but the sound in the pub was strangely muffled with a 'flat' quality. There were perhaps 20 people in that room but there was no chatter or background noise. It was so subdued and just not right. The only way I can describe it was like a noisy pub with the sound turned down. Some of the old men were playing cards. Just behind them were a couple of old one-armed bandits. Not the flashing electrical ones you have in pubs today, but enormous machines with a single big handle at the side."

When Wendy and Gary sat down, the place went quiet. They felt every eye in the place turned towards them. "It was horrible; just so unfriendly. We think the pub must have been close to a village because everyone there seemed to be farmers or farm workers. Some of the old men wore caps and were smoking pipes or very smelly cigarettes. Most were drinking pints. The women wore long pinafore aprons or calf-length skirts. I was wearing jeans and a tee shirt, and felt uncomfortable as the only woman there in trousers," added Wendy.

'It wasn't Scary, just Weird'

"We sat at a wooden table with a gingham table cloth, sipping at our drinks. We only stayed long enough to drink up, a quarter-of-an-hour at most, and then we left. It wasn't scary, just weird; as if we had stepped back in time. But it wasn't until we were outside again and back in the car that we realised just how strange it was in there. The road was still empty and as we turned onto it, Gary and I looked at one another and simply shook our heads in disbelief.

"A few minutes later we drove into Brighstone. Suddenly there were cars, people and a sense of life and activity again. It was as if we had woken from a dream."

The strangeness of that experience has stayed with Wendy and Gary to this day. They have never been able to find the pub since, and don't even know what it was called. All they do know is that early one summer's evening they found a pub that doesn't exist and shared an uncomfortable drink with people who live in a different time or dimension. Is this experience the result of a timeslip, perhaps, or simply an overactive imagination? Or more mysterious still, could it have been an accidental journey into a parallel universe?

A current theory in quantum cosmology, postulated by noted scientists such as Professor Stephen Hawking and Nobel Prize winning physicist Steve Weinberg, suggests that ours is not the only universe, but is part of a much larger "multiverse" of parallel universes, which is truly timeless. In her book 'The Convoluted Universe', Dolores Cannon explains it thus:

"The theory is that an infinite number of universes could exist side by side with ours, but because they vibrate at different speeds, they are normally invisible to us. These universes intersect with each other, but usually these points of intersection aren't compatible and inhabitants of the different universes are not aware of this interaction.

However, occasionally people do cross over into another universe, which is so similar to ours as to be almost identical. When universes are overlapping in this way, people can cross temporarily for a short period of time and then back with no ill effects. They would not be aware of crossing, and would not be able to tell where one universe begins and the other ends but they would know that something is 'not quite right'.

They might remember something odd that happened while they were over there, but would think they had imagined it and forget the incident. Usually such crossovers are for short periods and generally people just continue with their lives and everyday activities, unaware they have crossed over and back.

Sometimes they might notice a particular building that exists where they have never seen one before. When they return to look for it, they can never find it again."

This sounds familiar doesn't it? As noted scientist J.B.Haldane observed: "The universe is not only queerer than we suppose, it is queerer than we can suppose."

THE LADY FROM THE CUPBOARD

One of the oldest and quaintest pubs on the Isle of Wight must surely be the Crab Inn, near Shanklin Chine in the Old Village. Steeped in history, with its thatched roof, flagstone floors, wood panelling, gleaming brasses and old-fashioned roses twining around the door, it is the epitome of a traditional English inn. For it to be haunted as well seems almost too good to be true. Over many years a white lady has been seen in part of the original building, where at a certain table, customers remark on the sudden chill which catches them unawares.

Tina and Derry Derbyshire took over as licensees at the Crab Inn in 1989 and James, their son, was born there. At the age of three he began to talk about 'the lady from the cupboard' explaining to his startled parents that he had a new friend; she was a lady in a white dress and she came through the cupboard.

"I am personally sceptical about the whole thing," said Derry. "But when we first took over the pub, a member of staff told us that the flat above the bar was haunted and that the ghost was known as 'Charlie'. An assistant manager here (who has since died) said he had seen the spirit of a young woman in the bar and also upstairs in the flat on several occasions. Wearing a maid's uniform, the ghost appeared to be of a white and misty substance.

"Over the years, sometimes months apart, customers have asked 'Have you got a ghost?' They go on to say they have just seen her or felt

A late nineteenth century photograph of the haunted Crab Inn, then an hotel

her. They remark on a sudden sensation of cold and of seeing a woman's figure - in white - walking towards the wall. It always happens in the same place, the oldest part of the pub, which is directly under that bedroom with the cupboard… where my son saw the white lady."

Prior to 1989, the Crab Inn was in the same family for 43 years. George and Gladys Bunn moved there in 1946, and later, when their granddaughter Sally Cooper was born, she spent much of her early childhood there. Sally's parents also ran a pub, the White Lion at Arreton, and her aunt and uncle, Audrey and George Moore, took over as licensees at the Crab Inn in 1959.

Sally recalls, "As soon as they moved in, items were moved and went missing. My aunt and her family called the presence 'Charlie' although I believe there may well have been more than one spirit present there. Charlie clearly disapproved of the alterations my aunt and uncle made to the old kitchens and cellars in 1960 and for months there were many strange accidents there, such as the time my great-grandmother crushed her fingers in a mangle and someone fell down the cellar steps. There were other accidents too small to mention, which were odd all the same.

"On a lighter note, my cousin Dave Moore who was helping to bottle up the bars came back through the cellar and dropped a bottle of Scotch, which instantly drained through the old flagstones as though it was being sucked down. Charlie went to sleep for quite some time after that!

"On numerous occasions after closing time at night, family and staff have seen 'something' walk through the old Public Bar when it was deserted. One family member was going between bars one night when she accidentally bumped into a ghost and felt its cold presence move through her body.

"After closing time one night, Dave's wife Sue was out taking the dog for a walk at about 11.30pm, when she noticed a lady in a long gown walking down Chine Lane.

"When the figure reached a little stream, which crosses the lane, it vanished. The dog's walk was cut very short that night, and Sue later discovered she had apparently seen the Grey Lady said to haunt the Old Village after her tragic death on her wedding night in Victorian times.

"Back at the Crab, one member of staff would never willing go into the upstairs laundry room where she complained that something there breathed on her neck.

"I well remember that room which had a very forbidding atmosphere. Many times as a child I stayed at the Crab and I still recall the ancient creaky corridor upstairs and a very strong feeling of being watched there by something in the shadows," said Sally with a shiver.

"In 1972 when David and Sue were living at the Crab, Sue gave birth to their daughter, Samantha. When they brought the new baby home from hospital, Sue took her upstairs to their bedroom.

"As she approached the door with the child in her arms it opened for her. This continued every day for three months - always happening at 11am each morning - when Samantha was taken up for a little sleep.

"After Sue had recovered from her initial shock she grew accustomed to that door opening for her and the baby and would say 'thank you Charlie' as she walked into the bedroom. As she did so, the door would close gently behind her.

"There was nothing unnerving about this, it was actually a gentle, comforting presence and Sue has often thought that the period of three months that this continued for was most significant. For she had lost Wendy, her first child, at the age of three months..."

A GHOST LINGERS AFTER TIME

The spirit of a young woman dressed in a long, white dress has been seen lingering at a Ventnor pub where she glides up and down the stairs, long after 'Time' is called. Wendy Lacey of Upper Ventnor saw the solid-looking apparition on several occasions when her former father-in-law was landlord at The Blenheim in Ventnor High Street.

The first time she saw the apparition, the ghostly figure was standing at the top of the stairs. Wendy recalls, "She had blondish hair, a full-length white dress with layers and layers of silk, gathered at the waist with a deep sash. The young woman was in her twenties and I watched in astonishment as she started to move downstairs towards me, then vanished.

"In those days I remember the old pub felt so cold that I always took a coat with me when I went there - even in the summer."

Originally the pub, which until the turn of the century was a Burt's property, had four bars. One of these on the first floor, known as the Birdcage, was evidently the permitted 'haunt' of the ladies. (Perhaps the ghost in the silk dress was once one of these patrons).

Below ground are extensive and beautifully constructed cellars extending some 50 yards back from the High Street, containing numbered bays for wine vats and a deep well. There is another well in the rear courtyard, and the lady in white has also been seen standing here, before she disappears into thin air.

Landlord Michael Askew hasn't seen the ghost himself, but he's heard stories about her from his regulars at the Blenheim. "She's been mentioned from time to time. I won't mind if she puts in an appearance. We serve all kinds of spirits here," he said. Pub regulars Ray and Laurie Durham recall that when Tim Saul, who ran the neighbouring Volunteer pub, also leased the Blenheim, he saw a ghost walk through a sealed up door in the cellars. "He appeared in the bar looking white as a sheet and very shaken. He told us he had seen a solid-looking man walk across the cellar corridor and disappear through a door which was locked and sealed. Down in those cellars, where old smugglers' tunnels are said to run, the sound of barrels moving at night has also been heard.

"Cleaners have been surprised to see the odd customer sitting at the bar when they arrive early some mornings," added Laurie. "They are certainly odd, for these are no ordinary customers but ghosts - who quickly disappear. Perhaps it's their turn to buy a round," he laughed.

UNWASHED SPIRIT AT THE BUDDLE

In June 2003, Jean and Dave Moule stayed at a cottage at Castlehaven, near Niton, which happily for them, was close to the charming and historic Buddle Inn. Not so charming however was Jean's encounter with a rather smelly spirit – and it wasn't even the bottled variety!

Jean explained, "The first night we went to the Buddle we sat to the right of the bar, and although the place wasn't busy, I started to sense we were being watched. I was aware of an unseen presence near the small fireplace. We decided to take some photos with our new digital camera, but couldn't get it to work. The battery was apparently dead, even though it had been fully charged that day. Ten minutes later however, the camera decided to work and we took our pictures. At that point I also noticed the feeling of a presence had gone.

"The second night, Dave and I sat down opposite each other at a four-seater table, near the inn's large fireplace. I went to order the food while Dave visited the Gents. We both returned to our table together, and as I went to take my seat I noticed one of the chairs, which was previously tucked well under our table, had been pulled right out. I asked Dave why he had done that. He replied 'I thought you must have done it'.

The historic haunted Buddle Inn at Niton Undercliff

"Although there was no one else nearby, I started to feel a strange presence again and a strong, unpleasant odour around me. It was a really strong, rancid smell of old body odour and stale tobacco, as if someone hadn't washed for weeks. Dave, however, couldn't smell a thing!

"To escape the smell I went to play the pub fruit machine. I decided to gamble £2 and keep any winnings. To my surprise I won and returned to the table with a handful of £1 coins. At that point our food arrived and I suddenly noticed the smell had gone.

"After we finished our meal, Dave counted my winnings. 'I don't believe it, you have only gone and won enough to cover the food bill, again,' he laughed. (This is not something I normally do but on the previous evening I had also gambled £2 and won £13; which was just enough to cover that food bill) This may have just been a coincidence, but it was odd to say the least!" said Jean.

The Buddle, which sits on the cliff top overlooking St Catherine's Lighthouse, started life as a three-room farm cottage in the sixteenth century. The inn's exact age is unknown, although it was granted its first licence in 1850.

It had been operating as an unlicensed alehouse for many years prior to that and farming continued there until the First World War. The Buddle stream which rises in the back yard, always 12 degrees colder than the tap water, was once used for watercress beds and more importantly, for cooling beer.

Here, on a wild and stormy winter's night, while snug in the cosy old inn with its stone-flagged floors, dark beams and massive open fireplace, tales of ghostly smugglers, wreckers and phantom fishermen don't seem so far fetched.

After 17 years as the Buddle's landlord, John Bourne has heard a number of ghost stories at the old inn, and although he's never seen any unwelcome spirits himself, some visitors certainly have. "Over the years, several people have talked of seeing figures walking from the fireplace across the bar and into the end wall on the Ventnor side of the pub. One lady was so spooked that she refused to stay," said John.

"Although I don't really believe in such things myself, it's remarkable that so many of the descriptions do match. People see the ghosts of long-dead smugglers, sailors and customs men, wearing very old-fashioned clothing, with hats and long jackets, passing through the bar. Although whether any of them also has B.O. I've no idea!"

WIGHT SPIRIT – BREWED SUPERNATURALLY!

The ghost of a long-dead brewer who still keeps a watchful eye over the beer-making has had a modern-day ale created and named Wight Spirit in his honour.

Wearing old-fashioned clothing, complete with starched wing collar and rolled up shirtsleeves, the phantom brewer has been seen at a third floor window, once the labelling room, surveying the yard at Ventnor Brewery, while his spirit is also heard whistling in empty rooms.

There's been a brewery on the site since 1840, when Ventnor Brewery was opened to take advantage of the remarkably pure spring water, which rises through the chalk hill of St Boniface Down behind. A most favourable agreement with the Ventnor Water Company secured an unlimited supply of water for 1,000 years for just 6d (two-and-a-half pence) a year! The arrangement is still in force today, but with an additional £250 annual fee for the extraction licence.

In 1860 it was renamed Burt's Brewery, and for more than a century Burt's beers were drunk in pubs and inns throughout the Island. At one time there were no fewer than 148 breweries on the Isle of Wight - and of these 44 were actually in Ventnor! Of course they included many tiny brewhouses, many of whose ales were of indifferent quality and strength, but the variety would have gladdened the heart of many a CAMRA (Campaign for Real Ale) enthusiast today.

For almost a century, Burt's Brewery was owned and managed by generations of the Phillips family. In 1992, a national chain bought Burt's and operations were transferred to Newport. Today, a mainland brewery owns the name.

For six years the premises lay derelict. However, when brothers Xavier and Airon Baker re-opened the brewery with Bob Simpson, they reverted to the original name of Ventnor Brewery.

Built as a Victorian tower brewery, which used gravity to brew the beer, the building was damaged during a low level air raid on 18 August 1942, which left three local people dead. On 17 January 1943, two German Focke Wulf fighters flew in at sea level - so low that one severed telephone wires - to drop two 500kg bombs on Ventnor. Their target was the radar station on St Boniface Down behind the town, but the 'tip and run' raid devastated the town instead. One bomb demolished several homes, businesses, an hotel, and damaged at least 200 other properties. The other cut through the gable of St Boniface Villa, ricocheted onto the back of a radio shop, exploding on the lawn of the house next to the brewery - the Phillips family home, where tragically Jack Phillips' wife Mary, and his father William (Bill) Phillips were both killed instantly. His youngest sister, Pamela died later from her injuries.

Although rescue work continued through the night, a total of seven local people were killed in that raid. So do wartime events shed any light on the haunting at the brewery? "No-one knows who the ghost is, but there has been talk of one here for years," said Xavier. "I think that whoever he is, he's benign and friendly. The spirit was

They've been brewing ales at Ventnor Brewery since 1840!

seen recently by a young woman visitor who noticed a man, wearing old-fashioned clothes, standing at the top floor window with his sleeves rolled up, as if ready for work. We sometimes hear him whistling when the building is empty, and he has also been seen waving from the window of a disused storeroom which has always been known as Mocher's Room."

Who Mocher was or why the room was named after him is not known. Does he haunt his old workplace? Whoever the ghost is, he still likes his ale and clearly has no time for other beverages. When Xavier and Airon bought some traditional cider with a view to selling it as part of the Ventnor Brewery range, they found the three stone flagons had been thrown across the room and smashed.

"It couldn't have happened by accident. It was done deliberately in the night and when we found the broken the jugs next morning, I think he was trying to tell us he didn't approve of cider in his brewery!

"Apart from that we have had no trouble with him," said Xavier. "I really feel that he's happy the brewery is back in business again and he's keeping an eye on things. We have even named a beer in his honour now. We call it our Wight Spirit bitter – Brewed Supernaturally. I don't know if he still approves of what we're brewing here today, but at the dead of night when all is quiet, it would be nice to think he enjoys a sup or two!"

Chapter Thirteen

LIGHTHOUSE SPIRITS AT ST CATHERINE'S

Below the haunted Buddle Inn at the southernmost point of the Island stands St Catherine's Lighthouse. This white octagonal tower has 94 steps to the lantern, whose beam can be seen by ships up to 26 nautical miles away. At almost one million candlepower it is the third most powerful light in the Trinity House Service. Now unmanned and controlled from Harwich, the lighthouse has been automated since July 1997, although it is still open to the public at certain times between June and October, with tours licensed by Trinity House.

There has been a lighthouse at Niton since 1323, when local landowner Walter de Godyton was ordered by the Church, as a penance, to build a lighthouse on St Catherine's Down and pay a priest to say Masses for the souls of shipwrecked mariners who came to grief on this dangerous coast. A brazier in the 35ft high octagonal tower was kept burning, and the remains of St Catherine's Oratory, known locally as the Pepper Pot, can still be seen today.

As a lighthouse however, it wasn't a great success, for frequent thick fogs obscured the feeble light and ships still foundered on the treacherous rocks below. The wreck of the Clarendon in Chale Bay in 1836 with the loss of 24 lives so shocked public opinion that a new lighthouse, near sea level at St Catherine's Point, was started in 1838.

The original tower, which stood at 120ft, was too high, for fog still obscured the light, so in 1875 it was reduced to just 86ft. In 1932, the St Catherine's foghorn with a range of ten miles was moved from the cliff edge to a low replica tower in front of the lighthouse and these two towers are known locally as the 'Cow and Calf'. The foghorn was discontinued in 1987.

St Catherine's Oratory, Niton

St Catherine's lighthouse pictured in the 1920s

The lighthouse has been continually in service since 1875, although during the last war its light was extinguished to prevent enemy bombers using it for navigation and only lit when convoys were due to pass. Tragedy struck on 1 June 1943, when the very last local air raid of the war nearly put out the light forever. The damage this raid caused to the original 1840 lead crystal reflector glass can be seen to this day, as can the poignant last entry in the watch keeper's log.

Eight Focke Wulf 190s launched a surprise attack on Niton, coming in at sea level that misty morning. Their target was probably the radar and wireless stations located there. But the large Undercliff Hotel, where service personnel were billeted, was completely demolished instead, with the loss of two lives.

At the nearby lighthouse the death toll was higher. A bomb which missed its target fell instead on the emergency power house and boiler room, where the keepers were stacking bird perches they had just taken down from the tower.

Tragically all three men, R.T.Grenfell, C.Tomkins and W.E.Jones were killed and lie buried together, in a single grave, in the local churchyard at Niton. A polished brass memorial to them is displayed in the main lighthouse tower.

FIGURE IN THE TOWER

St Catherine's lighthouse and Tower Cottage from a pen drawing by W. H. Bartlett

British Telecom engineer Les Fletcher wasn't aware of those events fifty years earlier when he arrived to install a new phone system in the lighthouse one winter's day in the early 1990s. "I was working there alone and the Keeper, Frank Creasey, left me to finish and lock up when I left. It was late in the afternoon and growing dark when I tested the system, collected my tools, and left the empty tower, locking the door behind me. I thought the lighthouse looked quite dramatic in the gathering dusk, so when I reached my van I found my camera and shot off a couple of photographs a few seconds apart."

It wasn't until Les had the film developed that he noticed something odd at the top of the lighthouse, which appears in the second of the two prints. Outlined against the window of the tower stands the dark figure of a burly man.

"I couldn't believe my eyes," said Les. "There was no one else in that tower with me and when I locked the door I know the lighthouse was empty. I have puzzled over those photographs for years but can't explain them. Reluctantly I have come to the conclusion that it's a ghostly keeper who stands there… and he's still on watch."

Author's note: The photographs were taken with a 35mm camera (not digital) and I am in possession of the negatives. These have been examined by experts, who have confirmed that they have not been tampered with in any way!

This photo was taken late one winter's afternoon by BT engineer Les Fletcher

NOISY GHOST FAMILY

When Frank Creasey examined those photographs in July 2004, he too, was puzzled by the strange figure in the tower, especially as he remembered Les working in the lighthouse and confirmed that he had been there alone.

A keeper with Trinity House for over 30 years, Frank has served at several of Britain's best-known lighthouses, including those at The Eddystone, Longships, and Needles. He moved to St Catherine's Lighthouse as a keeper in 1985, and after the lighthouse was automated continued there as an attendant, living in the house at the tower base with wife, Shirley.

Although he's been alone in the tower many times, Frank has never

This photograph, taken just moments later, has a ghostly figure in the tower!

seen that phantom figure. He does however admit to sharing his home with a noisy family of ghosts! Lighthouse Dwelling as it's known, was originally the battery house and tower entrance. After the wartime tragedy it was converted into the Principal Keeper's house – although it was still the tower entrance and a thoroughfare for visitors.

It's here, in their hallway, that Frank and Shirley hear, but never see, the ghosts of a man, woman and young girl playing out a small domestic drama. "We hear the mother talking to her daughter in a low voice. We cannot make out the words, but from the urgent tone of her voice she is clearly trying to hurry the little girl up. We then hear her trying to pull the child to the door, but the girl is protesting because she wants to wait for her father. Then come the sound of a man's footsteps following behind. All three go out of the front door and it slams shut.

"That front door is locked and bolted, but we still hear it slam when the ghosts leave. It's so odd. We only hear them leave and it's always the same, rather like a sound loop, which replays at intervals. Sometimes we can go for a year or more without hearing them. There's no recognisable pattern; it doesn't happen on any particular date or time of day. Although we can't make out the words, we have heard them so often over the years that we can almost understand what's being said.

"It doesn't worry us at all. Although we don't see the ghosts we know when they are about because our cat watches them, staring fixedly as they move around the living room and hall. The only time we have ever seen anything was when we bought a swing-top rubbish bin for the sitting room. They didn't like that. We would be in there of an evening and that lid would start swinging. They would play with it all the time. Finally, while we watched, the bin was kicked over. We got rid of it after that," Frank said.

Caught on Camera

As well as appearing in Les Fletcher's photograph, one of the lighthouse ghosts was captured on CCTV early one morning. Frank explained, "One morning in the summer of 1999, a young chap called round to apologise in case he had disturbed us during the night. The man, who was staying in a nearby caravan site with his brother and girlfriend, had been to a party the previous night. After a few drinks they had decided to have a look at the lighthouse. Just after 1am, while trying to get over the wall, his brother had fallen and the others had climbed over to help him."

They were sorry if they had made any noise which woke Frank, and wanted to apologise for trespassing too. But Frank already knew what the nocturnal visitors had been up to, for he had observed their drunken antics on the lighthouse security cameras.

"I could see all four of you quite clearly lit up in the spotlights. I even watched you lighting a cigarette," he laughed, and then added, "Who was the fourth chap with you?"

"There were only three of us," the visitor assured Frank. So to settle the matter, Frank showed him the security video. Four people - three men and one woman - were clearly visible on the film. However, while the three party-goers could be seen scrambling over the wall, the fourth figure, that of a man in dark clothes, appeared around the corner from the front door of the lighthouse to join them, before walking off towards the wall again.

"I don't know who on earth that was!" said the young man in astonishment. "There were only the three of us there," he insisted. "We never saw him at all, yet on the video he's standing right next to us. That's weird. Perhaps you've got a ghost here," he joked.

There's many a true word spoken in jest….

THE END

THE AUTHOR

Hundreds of ghosts, spirits, spooks and apparitions, haunt the Isle of Wight - the world's most haunted island. Powerful unseen energy or 'ley' lines run under this British island, just 70 miles from London, which attracts ghost-hunters and enthusiasts from all over the world.

Gay Baldwin started researching and recording ghost stories here in 1977, when the first book, *Ghosts of the Isle of Wight*, written with Ray Anker was published. There's no shortage of hauntings on Ghost Island, and *More Ghosts of the Isle of Wight*, *Ghosts of the Isle of Wight III*, *Isle of Wight Ghosts Book 4* and *Ghost Island* have also been best sellers.

Gay devised the popular Ghost Island walks; a range of historical walks with a supernatural slant, which have introduced thousands of Islanders and visitors to the darker side of places like Newport, Cowes, Appuldurcombe and Ventnor Botanic Gardens.

Although not psychic herself, as a journalist, who is also a member of the Ghost Club Society, Gay has interviewed many hundreds of people who have incredible and inexplicable experiences of hauntings. Armed with the facts, she then researches the history of the sites or houses involved, looking for logical reasons for the ghostly happenings. Some accounts defy rational explanation and this sixth book of Isle of Wight ghost stories will give even the most confirmed sceptic pause for thought.

Some of the things that go bump in the night are easily explained away. An over-active imagination can conjure up all sorts of "ghostly" sounds, smells and apparitions. Creaking timbers; skeletal branches tap tapping on window panes; owls or bats in flight after dark; mice or rats scurrying through attics or behind walls, can be the innocent origin of many a ghost story. Not in **every** case however....

After more than twenty-five years of writing about ghosts, Gay firmly believes in the supernatural. Too many people, reasonable, rational, sensible people, have had experiences and encounters which cannot be explained by anything other than the supernatural. Gay would like to hear any strange tales of ghosts or hauntings that you might have. You can contact her by e-mail on gb@hauntediw.demon.co.uk or on 01983 294651. You can also check her website at www.ghost-island.com for news, photographs and more new stories from the World's Most Haunted Island.

BIBLIOGRAPHY

AND FURTHER READING

Searle, Adrian - Isle of Wight at War
Brading, Rosetta - West Cowes and Northwood.
Jones, Jack and Johanna - The Isle of Wight, An Illustrated History.
Garle, Hubert - A Driving Tour of the Isle of Wight.
Tatem and Opie - A Dictionary of Superstitions.
Underwood, Peter - Ghosts and How to See Them.
Worsley, Richard - A History of the Isle of Wight, 1781.
J.W. Hill and Co, IW Directory, 1871.
Hickman, Tom - Death, A User's Guide, 2002.
Kokeritz, Helge - The Place Names of the Isle of Wight.
Eldridge, R.J. - Newport in Bygone Days.
Shepard, Bill - Newport Remembered.
Hassell - Tour of the Isle of Wight.
Wheeler, Raymond L. – From River to Sea.
Bullar, John - Guide to the Isle of Wight, 1821.
Cooke's Isle of Wight, 1813.
Winter, C.W.R. - This Enchanted Isle.
Cox, J.Charles - Country Churches of the Isle of Wight.
Albin - Companian or Vectiana, 1806.
Mitchell, Kevin - Newport Pubs.
Cannon, Dolores -The Convoluted Universe 2002.
Page, William – A History of Hampshire and the Isle of Wight, 1912.
Groves, John – An Historical Account of Cowes, 2002.
Williams, David L. – White's of Cowes, 1993.
A History of Newport Old and New, 2002.
Chambers, Vincent – Inns and Ale Bonchurch to Chale, 1986.
Isle of Wight Illustrated, Mates Guide, 1901.
Wheeler, Jack – History of St Thomas's Church, Ryde.
Reanney, Darryl – The Death of Forever, 1995.
Lethbridge, T.C. – A Step in the Dark, 1967.
Devereux, Paul – The New Ley Hunter's Guide, 1994.
Gauld, Alan – Mediumship and Survival, 1983.
Bro, Harmon – Edgar Cayce, A Seer Out of Season 1994.
McTaggart, Lynne – The Field, The Quest for the Secret Force of the Universe, 2001.

NOT SPOOKED YET?

WHY NOT ORDER YOUR PERSONAL, AUTOGRAPHED COPIES OF THE OTHER BOOKS AND VIDEO IN THIS SERIES. THEY ALSO MAKE THOUGHTFUL GIFTS FOR NERVOUS FRIENDS!!

Photocopy or send this order form to:

Gay Baldwin
9 Pine Tree Close, Cowes, Isle of Wight PO31 8DX
Telephone 01983 294651: e-mail gb@hauntediw.demon.co.uk

.... copies of Ghosts of the IW @ £4.95 each £............

.... copies of More Ghosts of the IW @ £4.95 each £............

.... copies of Ghosts of the IW, book III @ £6.95 each £............

.... copies of IW Ghosts, book four @ £6.95 each £............

.... copies of Ghost Island, book five @ £7.95 each £............

.... copies of Most Haunted Island, book 6 @ £8.95 each £............

.... copies of Ghost Island Video @ £12.95 each £............

Add £1.00 postage and packing for each book or video (eg 2 books & 1 video=£3.00 postage) **Postage** £............

TOTAL £............

Please make cheque/postal order payable to: Gay Baldwin.

NOTE: I usually dispatch orders the same or next day. Please allow two weeks before you panic. If a book *has* to be somewhere by a certain date, please tell me so that I can try to get it there on time. Let me know if you would like it signed. *Now also available – the Isle of Wight Ghost Hunter's Map at £1.00 each with postage at just 25p*

Name ....

Address ....

.... Post Code ....

Telephone .... e-mail ....